D1622604

CHRIST
LIGHT OF NATIONS

Eucharist and Evangelization

Conferences
of the International Eucharistic Congress
of Seville

Éditions Paulines

Vatican translation.

Phototypesetting: *Éditions Paulines*

Cover: *Mike Lory*

ISBN 2-89420-207-5

Legal Deposit — 1st Quarter 1994
Bibliothèque nationale du Québec
National Library of Canada

© 1994   Éditions Paulines
250, boul. Saint-François Nord
Sherbrooke, QC, J1E 2B9

CONTENTS

PREFACE

The celebration is indeed the culminating activity of a Eucharistic Congress but it should not be viewed as the crowning or final event of a long preparation. Rather, it marks a new beginning, as was the gathering in the Upper Room in Jerusalem on the day of Pentecost.

In response to our request, the Éditions Paulines have kindly agreed to publish in Canada, in this book, the major addresses given during the 45th International Eucharistic Congress. These addresses were received with great enthusiasm by the thousands of people who came from 80 countries to attend the Congress. They were delivered from 7 to 9 June 1993 in the magnificent Cathedral of Seville.

In the morning of the first three days of the Congress, addresses were delivered by the following: Cardinal Joachim Meisner, archbishop of Cologne (Germany), on the theme "Eucharist and Evangelization"; Cardinal Carlo Maria Martini, archbishop of Milan (Italy), on the theme "Eucharistic celebration, summit of evangelization", and Cardinal Jaime Sin, archbishop of Manila (Philippines), on the theme "Eucharist, the permanent driving force behind evangelization". The following spoke in the evening: Professor Guzman Carriquiry (Uruguay), under-secretary of the Pontifical Council for the Laity (Vatican), on the theme "Eucharist, source of an authentic Christian spirit"; Father Anthony McSweeney (Australia), former superior general of the Fathers of the Blessed

Sacrament, on the theme "Evangelizing riches of the Eucharist", and Sister Juana Elizondo Leiza (Spain), superior general of the Daughters of Charity, on the theme "Social demands of the Eucharistic participation and worship".

We have received numerous requests to have these addresses published, coming especially from the National Delegates, who hope to distribute them in their respective countries as a valuable tool for post-Congress work.

We recall and make our own the words of the Holy Father, proclaimed immediately after his arrival in Seville, before the Blessed Sacrament exposed in the Cathedral: "In union with me, ask Jesus Christ... to make the whole Church emerge from this Eucharistic Congress with a renewed strength to face the new evangelization of which the whole world is in such a great need... *Evangelization for the Eucharist, in the Eucharist and from the Eucharist*: these are three inseparable aspects of the way the Church lives the mystery of Christ and fulfils her mission of proclaiming it to all."

My wishes to all those who will read and meditate these pages are that they may have an increasingly better understanding of the evangelizing riches of the Eucharistic mystery. May they commit themselves to make these riches effective through a truly "conscious, active and prayerful" participation in the Celebration, the latter being interiorized by the contemplation and adoration of the Eucharist which also makes us perceive its social demands.

Rome, November 1993

Edouard Card. Gagnon, P.S.S.
President of the Vatican Committee for the International Eucharistic Congresses

EUCHARIST AND EVANGELIZATION

Cardinal Joachim Meisner
Archbishop of Cologne

Introduction

I think I should first try to define our subject a little more precisely, and especially the concept of "evangelization". There are of course abundant possibilities for evangelization. In his Apostolic Exhortation, Pope Paul VI says its main elements are proclaiming Christ to those who do not know him, preaching, catechesis, and conferring baptism and the other sacraments. He adds that "any partial and fragmentary definition which attempts to render the reality of evangelization in all its richness, complexity and dynamism does so only at the risk of impoverishing it and even of distorting it."[1] Evangelization is a vital process which embraces and requires man's whole life. The Second Vatican Council briefly describes it as "the proclamation of Christ by word and the testimony of life."[2]

But the Eucharist is not simply one aspect of evangelization among many.

---

[1] *Evangelii nuntiandi*, no. 17.

[2] *Lumen gentium*, no. 35.

In the most blessed Eucharist is contained the whole spiritual good of the Church, namely Christ himself, our Pasch and the living bread which gives life to men through his flesh — that flesh which is given life and gives life through the Holy Spirit. Thus men are invited and led to offer themselves, their works and all creation with Christ. For this reason the Eucharist appears as the source and the summit of all preaching of the Gospel.[3]

Accordingly, it is legitimate, indeed essential, to emphasize the connection between Eucharist and evangelization. In the words of the Psalms: "I go around your altar, O Lord, giving voice to my thanks, and recounting all your wondrous deeds."[4] Today after the Consecration we say: "We proclaim your death, O Lord, and we praise your resurrection until you come in glory." But the celebration of Christ's death and resurrection does not merely require proclamation, it is in itself the Gospel. Saint Paul the Apostle says to us: "Every time, then, you eat this bread and drink this cup you proclaim the death of the Lord until he comes."[5] A worthy celebration of the Eucharist proves to be sanctification and evangelization at the same time, for the Church as for the whole world.

Let us hear again the words of Pope Paul VI:

For the Church, evangelizing means bringing the good news into all the strata of humanity, and through its influence, transforming humanity from

---

[3] *Presbyterorum ordinis*, no. 5.

[4] Ps 26:6-7.

[5] 1 Cor 11:26.

within and making it new: "Now I am making the whole of creation new."[6]

Anyone who considers these words in terms of the Eucharist and evangelization will stop to think. Consecration of our offerings, consecration of creation. This connection is not a mere play on words but indicates God's aim and desire, which the Eastern Churches describe as "theosis", the deification of the world.

Thus, the Eucharist begins with God's incarnation. The Father surrenders his Son to the people, just as he will surrender himself through the Eucharist into the hands of the Church and by the same gesture delivers himself to the Passion. The Eastern Churches, therefore, present the events of Bethlehem Eucharistically. The place where Christ was presented to the world is not the manger but the altar on which the new-born child lies wrapped in swaddling-clothes, though they are put on crosswise to indicate the Mystery of the Cross that is inseparably linked with the Eucharist. Ox and ass as representatives of the heathen peoples and the Jews stand hungrily around the manger in order to eat their fill from its contents.

1. Substance

All living things, according to our knowledge and belief, are subject to the powerful impulse of self-preservation. It is expressed by the word "having." But the eternal life given us by the hand of God has a different connotation, that of sacrifice, the ability to offer one-

---

[6] *Evangelii nuntiandi*, no. 18.

self. And this kind of living is expressed by the word "giving." That is why, at the Last Supper, "Jesus took the bread, gave thanks, broke it and gave it to them, saying: This is my body, to be given for you."[7] And no one has a greater love than the one who sacrifices his life for his friends[8]. "Yes, God so loved the world that he gave his only Son..."[9] And finally Jesus, dying on the cross, says: "Father, into your hands I commend my spirit."[10] Then comes the soldier with the lance; he opens Christ's side and immediately blood and water flow out.[11] The blood of the Eucharist and the water of the baptism. The substance of Christ's life dissolves on the cross so that he can take from himself and give it to others. Jesus' way of life is not to preserve but to sacrifice himself.

All substance is present for transubstantiation, for God is love. This is no pious dictum but a reality conferred on mankind. "Through him all things came into being."[12] The original word of love is "thou". This God's first and true word is likewise "thou". When God speaks, his words are not empty phrases, but reality and truth. Hence the Father's eternal word is the Son. He is the paternal "thou" absolute. But because the Son is wholly the Father's Son, he speaks back to the Father in the original word of love. The love between Father and Son is itself a divine person, namely the eternal Holy Spirit.

---

[7] Cf. Lk 22:19.
[8] Cf. Jn 15:13.
[9] Cf. Jn 3:16.
[10] Lk 23:46.
[11] Cf. Jn 19:34.
[12] Jn 1:3.

Being love, God turns wholly "away from himself" and "toward others". In God exists not something static but a relationship, a "subsisting relationship", as the theologian would say, in other words, a love that has become a person. We see that, in revealing himself, the Father, for instance, never speaks of himself but refers only to His Son: "This is my beloved Son on whom my favor rests. Listen to him."[13] The Son in turn always draws attention away from himself toward his Father when he says, for instance: "[...] the Father is greater than I."[14] And when the Holy Spirit reveals himself, he never focusses attention on himself, always on the Father and the Son.

This likeness with God is our distinction as his creatures, it is both our mission and our Cross. For turning "away from oneself" and being totally focused "on others" crucifies. That is why the Lord says: "Whoever would save his life will lose it, and whoever loses his life... will save it."[15] Man much prefers to save his life than lose it. This is also reflected in the Eucharist, in which God has made it possible for himself to be given away in the form of Jesus Christ. It is comprehensible only in the light of the Passion.

If I love a person or thing, that person or thing becomes my Passion. To us humans, suffering and love are only different sides of the same coin. In God, however, it is love, not suffering. In the Most Holy Trinity, this turning away from oneself and being inclined toward others — this love — is total inspiration, total joy, total verticalness.

---

[13] Mt 17:5.
[14] Jn 14:28.
[15] Cf. Mk 8:35; Lk 9:24.

When this God became man in the form of his Son Jesus Christ, he described mankind with the form of the Cross. For man, marked by sin, is turned totally away from others toward himself. He is totally withdrawn from the community into isolation. He is totally earthbound in his horizontalness. But where the divine verticalness meets the human horizontalness, there is formed the Cross.

The Cross is therefore only the earthly sign of God's love, or of love in the human dimension. We are not redeemed by suffering, but by love, which, however, let me repeat, assumes the form of suffering in the earthly dimension. Man's likeness to God gives him a likeness to the Cross. Léon Bloy expresses this in his affirmation of God: "Lord, you pray for those who crucify you, yet you crucify those who love you."

And among the many names for God, one of the most appropriate is "wastrel". Our God is a God of wastefulness. He never gives just something, always himself. He never adds up the cost, he "forgets" himself when giving. This small host before which we genuflect is, in material terms, practically nothing, but it is his all. God has nothing more to give. "The bread I will give is my flesh, for the life of the world."[16] In the Holy Eucharist, we celebrate God's wasteful love. And truly human life emerges only under this symbol of waste which is incompatible with man's powerful instinct of self-preservation. That is why such life is only to be found under the Cross. The Eucharist is a fruit of the Cross. We are celebrating not only a meal, but first and foremost a sacrifice. The Cross became

---

[16] Jn 6:51.

the Tree of Life and the Eucharist the Fruit of the new Paradise.

We have long been taught that life exists in the things which man can own and consume. We are constantly informed of all the things we need to possess in order to become, at last, someone who matters. Where surplus prevails, we are told that we live only to consume. And where shortage prevails, we are told we live only in order to produce. But it makes no great difference whether we live in a consumer cooperative or a producer cooperative, for both of these blueprints for life conceal the same massive lie of this age: that man believes he can obtain what he needs for life from what can be brought about, what can be produced, what can be "had".

Just as Father, Son and Holy Spirit transcend toward one another in the Most Holy Trinity — and thus constitute the one God in three persons — man, indeed any form of existence, can only achieve consummation through transcendence or transubstantiation. Love in the worldly dimension always implies: foregoing self-love and giving preference to others, withdrawing oneself in order to give others more space. And the name for all this at all times is "Passion".

2. Transubstantiation

Because things are created in the image of the Son, they can, like the Son himself, be given away to others, be shared. In other words, they only fulfill the purpose of their existence if they refer beyond themselves to other things, to other people. This explains

15

why the opening words of the Consecration are: "This is my body — to be given for you" and "This is my blood — which will be shed for you."[17] This giving and this shedding refer unequivocally to the Crucifixion, which was anticipated by the Last Supper on Maundy Thursday. The Eucharistic day of freely giving oneself away, which began with God's incarnation, came before the events of the Passion and thus shows that Jesus' voluntary giving of himself is the existential reason why his subsequent brutal Passion signifies not tragic fate but universal salvation. This voluntary giving of oneself goes to the extreme, and the extreme is that the active disposing of oneself is transformed into a state of allowing oneself to be disposed of, a pure state of being at someone else's disposal. The passiveness of the Passion is a manifestation, a most active desire to sacrifice oneself which extends beyond the limits of self-determination into the limitlessness of allowing ourselves to be completely determined by others. This mission inherent in the Most Holy Trinity has its rationality in the will of each divine person to relinquish himself. The disposing of the Son in the Eucharist finds its justification in his allowing his fate to be determined by the Father. It is only in the Crucifixion that evangelization really begins.

Jesus' giving of himself to his own in the world reveals the giving of the Father, who, out of love for the world he has created and faithful to his covenant with it, sacrifices his most precious possession: his Son. Jesus' human reality is, by the very fact of his incarnation, Eucharistic to the extent that it is God's

---

[17] Lk 22:19; cf. 1 Cor 1:24.

personified gift to the world. In his suffering, Christ bows to the Father's will. Through the Eucharistic gift, he at the same time pierces the egoistic armour of the human heart. The process of transubstantiation begins. This is already indicated at the Marriage Feast of Cana, where the water was changed into wine. And finally, at the Last Supper in Jerusalem, Christ changes the wine into his blood. Those who partake of the chalice of consecration, of the blood of Christ, become part of his mystical body, which is constantly on the move proclaiming the joyous message.

But man has to allow himself to be blessed with his life. He cannot simply reach out for it as if for the Fruit of Paradise. He has to hold out his hands like a beggar. He has no legal claim to the Eucharist. Have you anything at all that was not given to you? For this bread is not at our disposal. It is by no means an "it", it is not something material; it is a "thou", a person — it is Christ himself! And one cannot possess a person; one can only make oneself available to a person. And that is why we have no right to dispose of life. We cannot decide on life and death. Letting someone live or die is not for us to decide; it is God's exclusive prerogative. What we can do is place ourselves at the disposal of all human life through the power of divine life. For, since Christ, all human life is no longer merely biological life but life protected by divine glory. This applies especially to the one who eats of this bread, for he has been promised: You will not see death in eternity[18]. We celebrate the presence of the Lord, of His divine life, in our midst and are thus celebrating the sanctification of human life.

---

[18] Cf. Jn 6:54.

This manifestation of Jesus' distribution of himself to his own in the Eucharist — and through them to the world — is an ultimate action. The word of the Father that has become flesh has been given for all time. It has been shared out by him and will never be taken back. The passage of Jesus' worldly form into its Eucharistic form lasts until the end of the world.

The risen Christ, too, bears his wounds as sources of the Eucharist on his glorified body. Jesus' self-surrender after sacrificing himself at the Last Supper, will never be reversed in the sense of self-disposal. Friedrich Engel's assertion that "man is what he eats" — that is to say, only substance — is basically untrue. It is true only of the Eucharistic meal: Christ is what he eats — that is to say, the body of Christ. Those who communicate, who become "one flesh", become part of that inner-trinitary movement "away from oneself toward others". He becomes part of this mission, which in the reality of this world mission, means evangelization. Evangelization thus exercises "its full capacity when it achieves the most intimate relationship, or better still, a permanent and unbroken intercommunication between the Word and the sacraments."[19] Only the one who is himself permeated with divine life can permeate the world with the same. Thus the Second Vatican Council teaches that "charity, which is, as it were, the soul of the whole apostolate, is given to them and nourished in them by the sacraments, the Eucharist above all."[20] Here one must ask: What is the relationship between the many com-

---

[19] *Evangelii nuntiandi*, no. 47.

[20] *Apostolatus laïcorum*, no. 3.

munions and evangelization in the current life of the Church?

Celebrating the Eucharist is not without danger. It can, in the words of Saint Paul the Apostle, become our judgment. Drawing attention to this danger is inconvenient, but if we forget it, the Eucharist easily becomes discredited. Saint Paul exhorts us to distinguish between the body of the Lord and ordinary food[21]. We could reassure ourselves by doing so. We kneel before the bread on the altar. We keep it in simple but precious utensils. We profess it to be vital for ourselves. That is right, but it is not sufficient. "Every time, then, you eat this bread and drink this cup, you proclaim the death of the Lord until he comes."[22]

So we see, the Eucharist celebrates the presence of the Lord, who sacrificed himself for us. Let us repeat it: this trinitary offering of his life by the Son to the Father, and vice versa, is, within the Most Holy Trinity, pure verticalness, pure happiness, pure joy, pure inspiration. But in the dimensions of a sinful world it means forgoing self-love, self-confirmation, it is a confrontation with our earthbound horizontalness, it becomes our Cross.

But the Eucharistic body, which we worship and receive, is therefore the body that was broken for us. Christ's sacrifice is among. The Lord's body is the monument to his active love in which he distributes his broken life among us. We are well advised to worship this bread, because it is from heaven, that is, from God. But those who worship, recognize. Yet our

---

[21] Cf. 1 Cor 11:27 ff.
[22] 1 Cor 11:26.

worship becomes a judgment against us if it does not evoke the decision that, with Christ, we accept the will of the Father and we ourselves wish to become a gift to our brothers and sisters in an intensive evangelizing movement.

We are well advised to eat the bread of life, because that is why it was given to us. But eating is appropriation, assimilation. Receiving the bread is testimony against us if it is not linked with the burning desire to become a part of Christ's way of life. Hence Christians should not be the "ultimate consumer" of the Eucharist, but must, for their part, be transformed into a Eucharistic existence which gives other people a share in their own life's substance, which is basically the substance of the life of Christ. Holy Communion means leading the lifestyle of Christ, who has gone the many ways of this world in order to preach the Gospel.

Therefore, young people who worship and receive the body of Christ, cannot at the same time merely ask what is offered to them without asking what is required of them. They kneel down before the one to whom the will of the Father is supreme. And if they worship the Lord, who gave his life for us, then men can no longer only want their wives, and wives their husbands, or parents their children, all to themselves. All of us only sincerely worship the body of Christ that was broken for many, only receive him worthily, if we do not merely think of our own interests, but of those of others who are waiting for the preaching of the Gospel. We, central Europeans, who have adequate medical care, can only receive the body of the Lord for our salvation if it opens us to the needs of others, so that we allow our wealth and our skills to be effectively used to help the poor and suffering of this world. After all, we are receiving the one who sacrificed himself and shared himself among us poor and needy.

He served us in order to make servants of us. By worshipping him and accepting his service, we assume obligations. Those obligations are not intended as a burden, however. The possibility of the Lord's body becoming our judgment should not deter us from receiving it. On the contrary, those who live only for themselves remain dead. For "to have", "to possess", "to retain" or "to want to gain", that is death. The death of Christ, on the other hand, and our dying with him as giving and losing, that is life. And the sacrificed Christ lives!

The Eucharistic celebration also proclaims the resurrection of Christ. I live and you too shall live. The body of the Lord has the power, the energy, to arouse, to nourish and to release in us his sacrifice — and thus his life. We must receive him for he can open us, detach us from ourselves and bind us to him and his mission for our brothers and sisters around the world.

He who eats this bread comes alive. The obligation to love, which we assume when we worship and receive the body of Christ, is not a burden but a "redemption". It allows us to live a worthy human life. Then our daily life becomes an indicator of the Lord's new life. Our life becomes a monstrance which we perhaps find much easier to create than the goldsmith who makes the precious receptacle that stands on our altars. But although the times when we, through this bread, have become a gift to the Father in heaven and a message to our brothers and sisters around the world, are but tiny treasures, they are the jewels which the Lord wishes to see decorating his body — his Church. For the bread is transformed, so that we become transformed with it into a worthy sacrifice for God and for the members of God's family among themselves who are called on behalf of those not yet called.

The substance undergoes transubstantiation and gives our life a dynamism that enables us to preach the Gospel to the world. The bread becomes the body of the Lord so as to build up as the body of Christ in this world those of us who eat it. Thus the success of the Eucharist depends on whether it makes us more alive, in other words, whether we grow in our missionary role. We have bread which enables us to give thanks and to love. It can have the effect that we can say from our own experience, like the first Christians, that "we have passed from death to life, we know because we love the brothers."[23]

3. Communio

All substance is present for transubstantiation, but transubstantiation is intended for communion. God is triune but he is only the *one* God. The Lord allows us to share his trinitarian and Eucharistic body, so that we become a body — his body — which we break and share out in the missionary work of our everyday lives.

The Church becomes the body of Christ through the Eucharist. It is the most close-knit system in the world, since it contains the infinitely minute particles of the Holy Sacrifice that is greater than the world. As

---

[23] 1 Jn 3:14.

the body of Christ, the Church is a total denseness and concentration of matter and hence capable of participating to the extreme in the sufferings of the nations. That is why it is "lumen gentium", the light of the nations.

Mission or evangelization will mean in the present circumstances, notably in Europe, sharing the faith, through Christ sharing his life. As bishop of priests in the archdiocese of Cologne, I am asked more than ever before, which catechesis should be given to families who come from the formerly communist eastern part of Germany to the western part, and now — in complete ignorance of the faith — seek admission to the Catholic Church. My answer is always that they cannot yet be given catechesis, that we have to find families who are willing to share their lives — and thereby their faith — for a whole Christian year, to spend Sundays and feast days, and at least some of their holidays, with them. It is essential for them to learn to think and live like people of the faith before, with the help of catechesis, they can reflect on their experience of the faith. It is tragic when people asking for faith are expected to reflect on something they have never experienced.

Faith has never been passed on through publicity and propaganda, always through "infection", as it were. To use a different metaphor, which begins negatively: anyone who comes into contact with radioactive material himself becomes radioactive, and then infects others radioactively. But we must put a positive interpretation on it. Anyone who comes into contact with the Eucharistic Christ, who is in communion with him, becomes "Christoactive", and all who come into contact with him are themselves filled with Christoactivity. The people crowded round Christ to be able at least to touch the hem of his garment because there emanated from him a power which healed all[24]. The people of Jerusalem brought the sick into the streets, because even the shadow of the apostles passing by made them well again[25].

Evangelization means providing the world with such dispensers of life, in other words making Christ touchable for the people. God left himself to the people in the form of Jesus Christ, his Eucharistic legacy, as it were. He wanted the sacrifice anticipated at the Last Supper to be a great feast, something of pure joy. Until then everything had been too complicated, too theoretical, too abstract. What good to the world was an intellectual religion which shows a God that one had to invent in order to believe in him, a God one had to understand rationally in order to recognize him?

God wanted to make himself wholly comprehensible in Jesus Christ. He has made the faith visible, tangible and enjoyable for us through the incarnation of his Son and his Eucharistic sacrifice. In the Eucharist, God enters us through all our senses. He is the God who enters us in the easiest, the most common and the most frequent way, a way which is best suited to our abilities and inclinations. God sought to enrich us with a joyous generosity that enables everyone to become an evangelist and missionary.

Just as the bread lying on the altar is made from the harvested wheat whose ears previously grew scattered on the hills, just as the wine on the altar is

---

[24] Cf. Mt 14:36; Mk 6:56.
[25] Cf. Ac 5:15.

prepared from grapes which hung on different slopes but are now wonderfully merged in one single wine, all who communicate are gathered together in one body. They become the body of the living Christ, the great body of the children of God.

When we have become that body, when we have taken our place and found our life in this body, we will realize that we must in turn offer and pass that body on to others, that we have become the body which all need in order to become pure, comforted and converted. That is how we too will offer this body.

Thus evangelization is not propaganda or advertising, but the consequence of creation and the Eucharist. All substance is present for transubstantiation and transubstantiation for communion. Transubstantiation takes place through the Mystery of the Cross, in that it frees us from ourselves, allowing us to serve our brothers and sisters. Anyone who, in the process of evangelization, excludes the Cross, will never achieve his aim. We are prevented from excluding it by the Eucharist, which, through the transubstantiation of the substance, bread has become the body of Christ sacrificed for us, to which there is no alternative and for which the people are waiting — often unknowingly.

THE EUCHARIST, SOURCE
OF THE TRUE CHRISTIAN SPIRIT

Guzmán Carriquiry Lecour
Under-Secretary of the
Pontifical Committee for the Laity

From the apostolic witness
in the tradition of the Church

"The bread that we break is the Body of Christ, and the wine his Blood. These two visible elements, sanctified by the Holy Spirit, are transformed into the divine sacrement."[1] This is how the Eucharist was described at the beginning of the seventh century by Isidore, a metropolitan bishop of the Spanish Church. How many times he had proclaimed and explained this sublime mystery from his *cathedra* here in Seville, which was well known, among other things as well, for promoting the splendour of the Catholic liturgy. Isidore was a leading figure at a particularly crucial stage of transition between the crumbling Roman Empire and a new world which emerged from its ruins, violence and heresies. He was to spearhead the new evangelization which would foster the endeav-

---

[1] Saint Isidore of Seville, *De ecclesiasticis officiis*, c. XVIII "De sacrificio," Tipographía Regia, Madrid, 1599.

our to build something founded on and sustained by Christ, the "corner stone".

The work of Saint Isidore echoes that of the entire patristic age — he is regarded as "the last of the great Western Fathers of the Chruch"[2] — for he built on and carried forward the tradition of the apostolic witness. Saint Paul himself, who came to Spain about 63-64 to proclaim the Gospel of Jesus Christ, had written a little earlier to the Christian community of Corinth:

> For I received from the Lord what I also delivered to you, that the Lord Jesus on the night when he was betrayed took bread, and when he had given thanks, he broke it, and said, "This is my body which is for you. Do this in remembrance of me." In the same way also the cup, after supper, saying, "This cup is the new covenant in my blood. Do this, as often as you drink it, in remembrance of me."[3]

The well known close connection between this pauline text and the accounts of the synoptic Gospels regarding the Last Supper and the Institution of the

---

[2] "He stands halfway between the great founding bishops of the Western Church and the great organizers and animators of the new world being born"; Saint Isidore was "a spiritual father of many generations and universal teacher of a millennium" (cf. J. Pérez Urbel, *Sancto Isidoro de Sevilla*, Ed. Labor s.a., Barcelona, 1945, p. 284). What he bequeathed influenced the "carolingian renaissance", in which his authority was invoked in the debates which shaped the doctrine of the Eucharist and eventually developed the concept of "transsubstantiation". Obviously at the time of Saint Isidore this word was as yet unknown. But this concept is implied in his teaching especially in the realism of his beautiful pages dealing with "sacrifice".

[3] 1 Cor 11:23-25 [RSV translation used for quotations from Scripture].

Eucharist[4], has its roots in the unique tradition of the earliest Christian community in which the disciples of the Lord "devoted themselves to the apostles' teaching and fellowship, to the breaking of bread and the prayers."[5]

Many centuries later the same apostolic tradition would be the vitalising influence of the Church in Seville at the time of the "Catholic Reform" following the Council of Trent. It would shape the eucharistic piety which played no small part in the evangelization of the new world of the Americas and was passed on to and shared by the newly baptized peoples there. Among these people the feast of *Corpus Christi* very quickly took on a particularly important significance. For their indigenous cultural practices of adoring and offering sacrifice to the sun as the focal point of their cosmic rituals became transformed once the true Sun was revealed to them and they acknowledged Jesus Christ as the Redeemer of mankind, the centre of the whole world and of all history.

Today, at the dawn of the third millennium of the incarnation of the Son of God, we are enlightened by the teaching of the Second Vatican Council, which often referred to the Eucharist as "the source and summit of the whole Christian life."[6] This teaching is emphasised as the central content that organically binds together the "*depositum fidei*" (deposit of faith) in the new *Catechism of the Catholic Church*, for which we

---

[4] Cf. Mt 26:26-29; Mk 14:22-25; Lk 22:14-20.

[5] Ac 2:42.

[6] Cf. *Lumen gentium*, no. 11; *Sacrosanctum concilium*, no. 10; *Presbyterorum ordinis* no. 5; *Christus Dominus*, no. 30; *Ad gentes*, no. 9.

are deeply grateful[7]. This is the context of our celebration of this International Eucharistic Congress, an event of grace in which we are called together to proclaim publicly with the apostles around Peter, with their successors, with countless saints and martyrs, confessors of the faith, evangelists and missionaries, what has always been believed and taught by the Magisterium of the Church and held by the *Sensus Fidei* of the people of God from generation to generation... namely, that the incarnate Word of God, Jesus Christ, who was crucified and gloriously raised from the dead, is truly, really and substantially present in the Eucharist under the signs of bread and wine. Great is the Mystery of Faith, the Sacrament of our Redemption!

An ever new challenge and witness

We are constantly required, however, to enliven this tradition which we have received, radically rediscover the heart of our Christian experience, sharpen our focus on the centrality of ecclesial communion, re-invigorate our missionary sense of responsibility. We can meet this multiple challenge only by participating with an ever greater and deeper awareness in the paschal mystery and the work of redemption which we celebrate in each Eucharist.

Our age is marked by instability, experimentation, confusion and restless searching for a new order; it is threatened by old and new kinds of slavery, which appear mainly as indifference, conformism and scep-

---

[7] *Catechismo della Chiesa cattolica*, Libreria Editrice Vaticana, 1992, nos. 1322-1420.

ticism. In such a situation today we remain like the disciples imploring the Lord: "Lord, to whom shall we go? You have the words of eternal life."[8] The Gospels relate, however, that when Jesus foretold his eucharistic sacrifice many left him, saying: *"This is hard saying; who can listen to it?"* It would be quite another matter, yesterday and today, if he were a religious leader, prophet, moral teacher, whose life and message were remembered merely symbolically in certain religious actions. But, the impact of his promise is evident in the astonished question: *"How can this man give us his flesh to eat?"*[9] It is difficult to recognize really that it is the same person who abides "nearest to the Father" in the Trinity, and also who, in the incarnation, is born of Mary[10] — the carpenter's son, born in Bethlehem almost 2000 years ago, who died on the cross and was raised from the dead: it is this same Jesus who remains a living Presence for people of all time and every place in giving his Body to be eaten and his Blood to be drunk."[11]

---

[8] Jn 6:68.

[9] Jn 6:51-58.

[10] [In Spanish there is a play on the words of Jn 1:18 — Vulgate: "in sinu Patris"; RSV: "in the bosom of the Father" — which are contrasted with "*en el sono* de Maria". Tr.]

[11] M.J. Scheeben draws this remarkable analogy: "Thus the mystery of the Eucharist is ontologically joined to the mystery of the Incarnation, just as the mystery of the Incarnation is joined to the Trinity. The Incarnation is the presupposition and explanation of the Eucharist, just as the eternal generation from the bosom of the Father is the presupposition and explanation of the Incarnation, regarded as the stepping forth of God's Son into the world." — Cf. *The Mysteries of Christianity*, (tr. Cyril Vollert S.J.) B. Herder Book Co., St Louis & London, 1947, p. 477 ff.

Is the Lord's statement perhaps not too hard also for our little faith as his unworthy disciples? We do not face up to it when we allow the distractions and mediocrity of our ordinary lives to reduce the profound significance of this infinite divine gift to the meagre limitations of our ideas and ways of thinking; when the wonder of such an unheard of and extraordinary event — demanding utter reverence, humble attentiveness, gratitude and praise, trust in its tender mercy — becomes obscured in being treated as a routine, traditional ritual duty, a matter of conventional practice or conformity; when we approach the eucharistic table in such great numbers while neglecting the sacrament of reconciliation; when what we celebrate in the church becomes in fact irrelevant to or divorced from our ordinary lives, which is the milieu to which the Eucharist directs us: *"Ite missa est... Go forth, you are sent out..."*

Look, friends, we are living in an age in which the Christian tradition is being corroded and harassed by "the goods and lords of this world". It is not enough to rely on the residue of a heritage which runs the risk of becoming dried up. More than ever it is true what a teacher of faith highlights in our time — that one must not presuppose faith nor take it for granted, but always return to expound the faith: *"Faith must continually be re-lived. And since it is an act embracing all aspects of our existence, faith must be also re-thought and always witnessed afresh."*[12]

---

[12] This is a quotation from Hans Urs von Balthasar on which Cardinal Joseph Ratzinger comments in *Che cosa crede la Chiesa*, (What the Church believes), "Il Sabato," Roma-Milano, 30 Jan. 1993.

The Fathers of the Second Vatican Council proposed in this regard a "return to the sources"; they asked themselves: *"Church, what do you say about yourself?"*, in order to proclaim from an entirely fresh starting point that *"Christ is the light of the nations."*[13] Today, thirty years after the Council, the question is still more radical. It is rooted in that very question which Christ put to the apostles — *"But you, who do you say that I am."* This is what confronts us today again and again in the most varied and concrete circumstances through which Providence seeks to win our "heart". This is the paramount question of our life. No other question that may present itself is more serious, more decisive than this. Our whole life — indeed, everything! — is at stake and depends on the response to this question. With Peter's enthusiasm and full conviction we reply: *"You are the Christ, the Son of the living God!"*[14]

This is what we desire to see as the fruit of this Congress: that the inexhaustible depth, beauty and richness of the mystery of Emmanuel, God with us, in the Eucharist be proclaimed afresh and relived. I suggest that we reflect today on the section of Pope John Paul II's first Encyclical Letter, *Redemptor hominis*, dealing with the Eucharist, where he presents it in terms of Sacrament-Presence, Sacrament-Sacrifice and Sacrament-Communion[15].

---

[13] *Lumen gentium*, no. 1.

[14] Cf. Mt 16:15-16.

[15] Cf. *Redemptor hominis*, 1979, no. 20.

Witnesses of a Presence

Saint Thomas Aquinas states that the Eucharist is the sacrament *par excellence* — the most important sacrament since in it Christ remains present not only in virtue of the gift of his grace, but personally. The New Testament begins by announcing that the Word became flesh and the Eucharist is the last, most profound, intimate and finest realisation of this event, which is God's gift to humanity of his presence, his companionship. "If the Word were not made man, we would not have his flesh", writes Saint Augustine, "and if we did not have his flesh, we would not eat the bread of the altar."[16]

"What indeed is Christianity? Is it perhaps a doctrine that can be taught in a school of religion? Is it perhaps a collection of moral laws? Is it perhaps a certain combination of rituals? All this is beside the point, coming afterwards. Christianity is a fact, an event."[17] It is, above all, a presence — the here and now of the Lord, who sustains us in the here and now of the act of believing and in the concrete reality of the life of faith. It is neither a theory, nor morality, nor ritual, but an event and, because of it, a real meeting with a Presence, that of God who has entered history and in the Eucharist is "the incarnate Jesus' flesh and blood"[18]. There is cer-

---

[16] Saint Augustine, *Sermon 130,2* — cited by Carlo Porro in *L'Eucharistia tra storia e teologia (The Eucharist — between history and theology)*, Piemme, Casale Monferrato, 1990, p. 41.

[17] Monsignor Luigi Giussani, *Un avvenimento di vita, cioè una storia,* (An Event of Life, that is a history), Ed. S.r.l., Roma, 1993, p. 338.

[18] Saint Justin, *Apol. I*, 65-67, cited in *La Teologia dei Padri*, Città Nuova ed., Roma, 1984, vol. 4, p. 159.

tainly no question of some nostalgic and pious remembrance of what took place about 2000 years ago, but of acknowledging in the light of faith his living Presence which always comes to meet mankind and which calls us to follow him today with the same reality, freshness and timeliness, attractiveness and tenderness that he showed when meeting and converting his first apostles and disciples in Palestine. Christ continues to invite us to follow him just as he did in calling Simon and Andrew, John and James, Mattew in the midst of their occupations. He wants us to experience his company as when he said to those two disciples of John the Baptist: *"Come and see"*; he comes to our home as when he went to that of Zacchaeus. He welcomes us with the same merciful love which he showed to Mary Magdalene; he knows the depth of our heart and desires our welfare just as he revealed his solicitude for the Samaritan woman. He extends his intimacy and friendship to us as he shared it with Lazarus, Martha and Mary[19]. Thus he goes on meeting us — to heal and forgive us, to be near us, to teach and guide us... We are like the disheartened wayfarers of Emmaus who after recognizing his Presence in the breaking of bread could then recall how their hearts burned at that meeting which was utterly decisive for their life's journey[20].

This is the Christian way. In the course of the most varied circumstances of life, in the seemingly most ordinary and daily meetings, in the thick of routine tasks, the Lord goes on revealing himself to us as a

---

[19] Cf. Mt 4:18-22; 9, 9; Lk 19:1-11; 7:36-50; Jn 1:38-39; 4:6 ff.; 11:1 ff.

[20] Cf. Lk 24:13-36.

most wonderful companion. This is what his disciples radiantly communicate in witnessing to his Presence. We must live and re-live this meeting, this discipleship, this recognition of his Presence, until we can address Him intimately as "thou", dwell with Him. This is the way of learning to discover how to welcome and acknowledge his Real Presence in the Eucharist despite the infinite wonder of this great mystery. Only then, thanks to his grace, the promise of Jesus is no longer *"a hard saying — intolerable language..."*

Yes, we are aware of having truly met him when we experience his living Presence as the deepest personal response to the need for meaning and fulness of life — that response to the hunger and thirst for love and justice, to the longing for reconciliation and happiness throbbing in our hearts... and which cannot be ultimately satisfied by this world's allurements to power, riches or pleasure. Thus the "new creature" is formed in us who by baptism are incorporated into Christ until we can say with the Apostle: *"it is no longer I who live, but Christ who lives in me."*[21]

The miracle of the transformation of a person's life, which is brought about by conversion to a more authentically human way of living through believing in Jesus and welcoming him in the Eucharist, is the greatest achievement witnessing to the truth of his Presence. Christianity thus takes shape not as an abstraction or theory, nor merely as a pattern of behaviour, but as a living, personal and social witness to the permanent presence of God who is One in our midst: Jesus Christ in his Church. He is the source and

---

[21] Cf. 2 Cor 5:17; Gal 2:19-20.

personal object of Christian experience as the presence of a friend, a father or mother; he is thus the ultimate horizon moulding the whole of life, the most decisive and richly creative vitality of love, the focal point in our way of regarding, understanding and confronting the whole of reality.

If we have met Jesus Christ and become his disciples, we are called to desire always that his Presence may be the vibrant and determining influence throughout our existence, giving it such a particularly evident radiant stamp that, despite our wretchedness, anyone meeting or living with us will ask: who are these people? How are they so fully human and yet so different? Wherever we may be — in the family circle, at school or university, in factories or offices, in every possible situation — if we make no impact on our neighbours, if they do not remain at least curious, moved perhaps only by a strange sense of wonder or attraction regarding our Christian presence... how are we to be credible in proclaiming the Presence of Christ in the Eucharist, to which we hope to bring others? If this were the case, then we must face the following disturbing and serious questions: have we ourselves truly encountered and become followers of Christ? Are we truly his witnesses by our lives? Do we indeed eat his Body and drink his Blood?... On the other hand, the living Presence of the Lord which changes our existence, which nourishes us in the Bread of his Word and his Body and Blood in the Church, illumines our vision and makes our hearts burn:

 • to recognize his Presence in the lives of other persons and all people;

• to commit ourselves to his Presence in that "other eucharist", namely the poor and suffering;

• to witness to his Presence in the entire gamut of our relationships;

• to proclaim his Presence as the sure promise of a new life to those who are caught up in struggling with life's pell-mell, searching and set-backs[22].

Handed over for our sins, raised up for our justification

The Eucharist is the Sacrament of the Real Presence of Jesus Christ who always comes to meet us. This means it is the Presence of his redemptive passover — the paschal Presence — in the *"flesh... which has suffered for our sins and which the Father has raised up."*[23] *"For as often as you eat this bread and drink the cup"*, — as the Apostle Paul says — *"you proclaim the Lord's death until he comes."*[24] The Eucharist is rooted in Jesus' death. The institution of the Eucharist and Jesus' death are at depth truly one and the same unique mystery. The prophetic gesture at the Last Supper in

---

[22] In this sense we become the "nourishment" for our brethren. Origen puts it this way in his homily on Lv 7:5 (Cf. *La Teologia dei Padri*, vol. 4, p. 169): "[...] in the second place, because of his flesh Peter and Paul and all the Apostles are a pure source of nourishment; in the third place, his disciples — and thus each one, in virtue of the quantity of his merits or by the quality of purity in his dispositions, can become wholesome nourishment for his neighbour [...]."

[23] Saint Ignatius of Antioch, *Ep. ad Smyrn.*, 7:1 — cited by C. Porro, *loc. cit.*, p. 153.

[24] 1 Cor 11:26.

offering his Body as "handed over" and his Blood as "poured out" for all[25] anticipates and presupposes as well as proclaims and interprets Jesus' imminent death on the cross. The Eucharist is the memorial of this perfect and definitive Sacrifice of the Word made flesh[26] — that Sacrifice which it calls to mind, re-presents, makes real for people of every place and time.

Jesus embraces every possible suffering of humanity; he is really burdened *"by the iniquity of us all."*[27] He is *"the lamb of God who takes away the sin of the world"*[28], an innocent victim, but one at the same time who surrenders himself. He offers his own life in obedience to and for the glorification of the Father; that is to say, he reveals his love for his Father and also the love for mankind which unites them. For the glory of God is the salvation of humanity.

As one great theologian wrote:

> The love which impelled him to surrender himself to death for us was also that which made him give himself as food. He was not satisfied in giving us his gifts, his words and counsel, but his very self. Maybe a woman, a mother, a lover can understand this need to give not something, but oneself — every fibre of one's being. This giving involves not only one's spirit or one's fidelity, but body and soul, flesh and blood — everything. Without a doubt the ultimate in love means seeking to nourish another with what one is. The Lord died to enter the state of his risen life in

---

[25] Ck. Lk 22:19; Mk 14:24.

[26] Cf. Rm 4:25; Gal 3:13; Ep 2:14-16.

[27] Cf. Is 53:2-6; Gal 3:14; Ep 2:14-17.

[28] Cf. Jn 1:29.

which he sought to share himself with everyone for all time[29].

Let us notice, brethren, that those *"hard sayings"* of Jesus imply the cross, which is the *"scandal"* and *"folly"* that Saint Paul refers to[30]. For we are always tempted to flee, to escape from those most awkward, but unavoidable questions which challenge our lives. We would prefer not to have to depend on the burden of creaturely limitation, nor to be subjected to the frustration of doing the very thing we do not wish to do and of not doing the good that we would like to do; likewise, we would prefer not to be trapped in the ambush of suffering, the boredom of work, the ambivalent instinct to possess those we love; or again, we would prefer to be freed from death, particularly the death to our loved ones and closest companions of a lifetime... We would wish that man were not a wolf to his fellowman, like Cain and Abel; that there be an end of exploitation, torture, violence, murder; that we were no longer estranged from one another. We even go so far as dreaming of a god who would not need the cross to love mankind. *"This is the horrible root of your error"*, Saint Augustine wrote, *"you pretend to make Christ's gift consist in his example, whereas the gift is himself, his very Person"*[31]. We preach a "crucified Christ"[32]. The language of the cross is not a myth, nor

---

[29] Romano Guardini, *Jesucristo*, Ed. Guadarrama, Madrid, 1960, p. 123.

[30] Cf. 1 Cor 1:23.

[31] Saint Augustine, *Contra Julianum. Opus imperfectum* — quoted in *Litteræ Communionis*, Milano, April 1990, no. 4.

[32] Cf. 1 Cor 1:23.

analogy, nor mere symbol, least of all a form of rhetoric.

But in our bodily existence, in the depths of our personality, in our social conditioning, in creation itself, there is a hidden longing which has not caused to exist in us: it is that desire not to remain subjugated to decadence; that yearning to be *"freed from corruption"* by the breaking of the bondage imposed by the power of sin and death. We anxiously await that liberation, that genuine fulfilment of our humanity in a happiness which is no longer weighed down by the burden of sadness. But, we cannot fulfil this longing by our own efforts.

Without Christ, without the Mystery which has conquered death[33], our whole life would be not only incomprehensible, but unjust.

All that I am, insofar as I am something more than a perishable being without hope, one whose illusions are all destroyed by death, I am because of that death which opens to me access to the God who fulfils me. I flourish in the tomb of the God who died for me; here my roots are deeply imbedded in the ground of his Flesh and his Blood[34].

There is no reason for anguish, then, but only thanksgiving. This is etymologically what "eucharist" means. What is primary, best and truest about us is knowing how to give thanks. For *"God so loved the world that he gave his only Son"* and *"he loved us to the end"*, *"greater love has no man than this, that a man lay*

[33] Cf. Col 1:18; Rm 8:2; Heb 1:15; Ac 2:24.
[34] Hans Urs von Balthasar, *Cordula, ovverosia il caso serio*, Queriniana, Brescia, 1968, p. 27.

down his life for his friends."[35] The mystery of the infinite love of God is revealed and reaches its zenith in Jesus Christ's self-emptying unto the Cross in all the depth and intensity of his suffering, his sacrifice, which was in function of something greater... It is a death leading to resurrection. It is a "passage" [*passover*] of Christ towards the Father and, with the glorified Christ, redeemed humanity's access also. Death and resurrection are no more than two facets of the same event of love.

Death has been overcome, brothers and sisters. But on one condition: without sacrifice there is no freedom, there is no liberation. There is nothing to fear about sacrifice — physical, moral, spiritual — because rather than being an obstacle to life, it is the condition of life. Because of sacrifice tenderness and happiness are rendered enduring, hope is enlivened, and every act of love becomes eternal. This is what matters. God is the ultimate purpose in living! Without sacrifice, there is and can be no genuine relationship of any kind — with one's wife, children, friends, or one's work. It is highly significant that during the Last Supper Jesus gave us the *"new commandment"* as the distinctive sign of his discipleship: to love as he has loved us[36]. Christ's love (*caritas Christi*) encourages and drives us on, since "if one has died for all" means that *"those who live might live no longer for themselves but for him who for their sake died and was raised."*[37] *"By this*

---

[35] Cf. Jn 3:16; 13:1; 15:13.

[36] Cf. Jn 13:34 ff.

[37] Cf. 2 Cor 5:14-21.

we know love, that he laid down his life for us; and we ought to lay down our lives for the brethren."[38] The only fitting way of showing gratitude for such great love is by surrendering one's entire life. We are called to martyrdom, and the *"world's hatred"* clearly reminds us of this[39].

Jesus wants us to be his collaborators in liberating the world by compassion for mankind. We are invited to take up the cross, to embrace and share human suffering, thus making up in our own flesh *"what is lacking in Christ's afflictions for the sake of his body, that is the Church."*[40] We cannot remain insensitive to Christ suffering especially in our most needy brothers. "We are with you", declared Pope John Paul II, "with all of you who bear in your own flesh the painful wounds of humanity today."[41] We are built up in the mystery of powerful solidarity by those who share in the suffering of Christ[42]. Let us be witnesses of compassion by suffering *with* our brothers and sisters, that is, passionately committed to defending their dignity and destiny. May we know to combat violence, injustice and deceit, which are concrete expressions of the world's sin.

We are living out, as it were, the pangs of childbirth: not merely in anguish, but aware also that a new humanity is being born. In the anguish of childbirth *"we possess the firstfruits of the Spirit"*; the adoption of the children of God is beginning to become

---

[38] Cf. 1 Jn 3:16.

[39] Cf. Mt 10:22; Jn 15:18-20.

[40] Cf. Col 1:24.

[41] John Paul II, *Christmas message,* 25 December 1984.

[42] John Paul II, *Salvifici doloris,* 1984, nos. 25-26-27.

evident, the *"redemption of our Body."*[43] By our relationship with Christ, that is, deepening our friendship with him through uniting ourselves with his sacrifice in the Eucharist, we realize that *"resurrection of the body"* has already begun as the dawning of a new day. Already, at every moment, we are being *"saved in hope."*[44] Hope is that certainty about the future which is fulfilled now, which begins to be realized or becomes real today. For this, *"we go on persevering in hope"* while our yearning is summed up in the exclamation with which the Bible ends: *"Come, Lord Jesus."*[45] In the meanwhile, however, as pilgrims we continue offering our lives together with the unique sacrifice of Christ on the altar through the ministry of the priest, and we are nourished by that daily bread for the journey which is *"the medicine of immortality, and the sovereign remedy by which we escape death and live in Jesus Christ for evermore."*[46]

Sharing — a mystery of communion

The Last Supper is the act in which Jesus establishes the Church by giving his disciples the liturgy of his death and resurrection. The Church celebrates its birth not only as an historical fact, but above all as an event which is constantly taking place and renewed in every Eucharistic sacrifice. The Fathers of the Church

---

[43] Cf. 1 Cor 15:20-24; Gal 3:26; Ep 1:15; Rm 8:14-17; 2 P 1:4; Ph 3:20.

[44] Rm 8:23 ff.

[45] Rev 22:20.

[46] Ignatius of Antioch, *Letter to the Ephesians*, 20:2; trans. in *Early Christians Writings*, Penguin Classics, 1968, p. 82.

developed the beautiful image of the Church — and hence of the Eucharist — as coming from the pierced side of Christ, from which flowed blood and water.

Christ's companionship in our journey through history is the Church, or rather his very Body. This is the manner in which his Presence is available to us today. The Church prolongs in time and space the real, living event of Jesus Christ: it is the means by which we become his contemporaries and he becomes our contemporary; it is the manner in which he comes to meet us throughout the most varied circumstances of life.

Credit is due to Henri de Lubac especially for drawing our attention to how the expression *"corpus mysticum" (Mystical Body)* originally referred to the Eucharist and that, for the Apostle Paul as well as the Fathers of the Church, the notion of the Church as the Body of Christ was inseparably bound up with that of the Eucharist[47]. From this there follows a eucharistic understanding of the mystery of the Church or eucharistic ecclesiology, which is often also called an ecclesiology of *communio*. This ecclesiology of communion is the heart of the Second Vatican Council's doctrine regarding the Church — a doctrine which is based both on the Church's reflection about itself and on its rediscovery of its roots.

There is a complete mutual penetration of the Church and the Eucharist as the mystery of communion becomes realized, deriving and flowing from the sacrifice of the New Covenant. Thus, it becomes clear that just as the Church *"makes the Eucharist"*, *"the*

---

[47] Cf. Henri de Lubac, *Méditation sur l'Église*, Aubier, Ed. Montaigne, Paris, 1954, p. 107 ff.

Eucharist makes" the Church[48]. By receiving Christ himself in eucharistic communion we remain intimately bound to the unity of his Body which is the Church. There is no bond more real, more intimate, more complete than this which unites us with Christ, and in Christ with the Trinity and with all mankind. By taking hold of us in baptism and in-corporating us in communion, Jesus Christ converts us into members of one single Body[49]. We are all one in Christ[50].

Whatever utopia has been thought up is far removed from this unity which Christ has actually brought about between us. If God has become incarnate — and is here present and communicates himself to us — then you and I are but one. Between you and me, who are strangers to one another, from different backgrounds, of various distinct cultures, something tremendous has happened: *tremendum mysterium.* We gratefully acknowledge ourselves bonded in a *"sign of unity and a bond of charity"*[51] which is much more powerful than any kind of family relationship or social, political or ideological solidarity. This comes about specifically because Christ is present through and within the miracle of our unity. We, you and I, have the sublime dignity and enormous responsibilty to be a physical sign of the reality of his Presence. What Saint Irenaeus long ago energically expressed against the gnostics of yesterday still holds good against the "spirituals" whose tendency is to flee

---

[48] Cf. *Redemptor hominis*, no. 20; *Lumen gentium*, no. 11.

[49] Cf. 1 Cor 10:15-17; 12:12,27; Rm 12:4-5; Ep 5:30.

[50] Cf. Gal 3:28; Col 3:11.

[51] Cf. 1 Cor 10:17, on which Saint Augustine comments in *In Evan. Joh.*, Tr. 31:13; cf. *Lumen gentium*, no. 7.

responsibility for the world: the Apostle Paul *"is not speaking about some spiritual and invisible man [...] on the contrary, he is speaking of the anatomy of a real man, consisting of flesh, nerves and bones, which is nourished by his chalice, the chalice of his blood, and gains growth from the bread which is his body."*[52]

This very fact, dear brothers and sisters, is the scandal which God provoked in becoming man, taking on the identity of the carpenter's son who claimed to be the Son of God, redeemer of mankind, centre of the cosmos and of history. An extension of this scandal is the Church. What are we but poor sinners who are chosen by God's mercy, despite our unworthiness, to be witnesses of that Presence which embraces all people since God *"desires all men to be saved and to come to the knowledge of the truth"*[53]? A community of sinners reconciled by the grace of God, which recognizes itself in faith as the Body of Christ, bears witness and proclaims the salvation of all people! This provoked the same rejection and persecution for the disciples as the Master suffered. It is easier and less risky to make ourselves acceptable to and curry favour with those of a wordly way of thinking. How often we make our own the image of the Church diffused by the worldly powers, especially through the mass-media, reducing the Church to suit their own purposes and interests. Thus, this image of the Church appears to be of interest for its moral norms and discipline for its theological discussions, for its political stance, for offering a "supplement of soul" to a materialistic

---

[52] Saint Irenaeus, *Adv. Haer.*, V.ii.2-3; translation in *The Divine Office*, II, Collins, 1974, p. 544.

[53] 1 Tm 2:4.

world... hardly for its spiritual or intellectual or moral aspects, which in reality, well beyond the limits of the press, are of interest to no one, in the sense that these matters do not "touch" the depths of any hearts or change anyone's life. We stay thus at a superficial level while what remains hidden and distorted is the witness to the living reality, to the central truth of the Mystery of the Word incarnate, bringing about a new unity for humanity. But, is the temptation within the Church itself perhaps not a similar one — namely when we remain obsessed with planning and making projects, organizing structures and tasks, in such a way that inordinate confidence is placed in our human resources and everything is viewed in a perspective of efficiency? On the contrary, it is through the gifts of the Holy Spirit, sacramental and charismatic that the grace of Jesus Christ is distributed; they build up and renew the Church, its communion and mission[54]. The Church is not "ours", it is God's! It has been rightly said that:

The Church cannot be produced, but only received, and it is received from where it already is, from where it is really present: from the sacramental community of Christ's body passing through history[55].

People do not become united as Christian community because of new undertakings, nor because of painstaking search for better means of organization, nor because of power-sharing or distribution of re-

---

[54] *Lumen gentium*, no. 4.

[55] Card. Joseph Ratzinger, "The Ecclesiology of the Second Vatican Council", *L'Osservatore Romano*, 27 November 1985; NC News translation in *Origins*, 14 Nov. 1985, Vol. 15, no. 22, p. 373.

sponsibilities. What truly gathers and draws them into one is a living reality, a newness of shared life such as is found in the Eucharist, its "source" and "summit". The Eucharist if the basis of the Church's spiritual, communal and missionary vitality[56]. It is the central sacrament of evangelization for which the world stands in urgent need[57].

Above all we must truly and lovingly welcome that gift of unity which is signified and guaranteed by communion with our Bishops who are united *cum et sub* Peter — communion which is both affective and effective[58]. All Christian communities are called to live and witness that mystery of communion — local churches, parishes and sanctuaries, fraternities and ecclesial movements, families and basic communities. All are called to become places of genuine personal development where one discovers his vocation and purpose in life; they defend one's freedom against the prevailing pressures; they foster growth to each one's true stature and a keen sense of responsibility for one's own and others' lives.

---

[56] "The encouragement and the deepening of Eucharistic worship are *proofs of that authentic renewal* which the Council set itself as an aim and of which they are *the central point*." — cf. John Paul II's *Letter to all the Bishops of the Church on the mystery of the Blessed Eucharist* (22 Feb. 1980) no. 3; translation in CTS Do519, p. 10.

[57] Cf. The Basic Text of the XLV International Eucharistic Congress, "Christ, Light of the Nations", nos. 11-15 in *Eucharist. The Heart of Evangelization*, Éditions Paulines, Sherbrooke, Québec, 1992, p. 28-37.

[58] The *Catechismo della Chiesa cattolica* (no. 893) says: "The 'Bishop is the steward of the grace of the high priesthood' (*Lumen gentium*, no. 26); this is particularly the case with the Eucharist which he offers himself or whose offering he assures through his co-workers, priests. The Eucharist indeed is the centre of the life of the local Church [...]."

That new life of unity is the greatest gift which God bestows on us for the conversion and transformation of the world. If we have truly eaten and drunk the Body and Blood of the Lord, we cannot live any longer estranged from one another but there must be a surprising brotherhood and friendship which we experience as spreading through the whole environment in which we live. We should provoke the same reaction as the early Christians and the martyrs did from the pagans: "See how they love one another!"

Our belonging to the Church, that is, our real communion is weak and fragile if, despite our sinfulness, it does not witness to the dawning of a new world of reconciliation — the first fruit of the unity and happiness for which the human heart yearns. It is not enough to say "Lord, Lord..." How can we proclaim that we share the bread of eternal life if we are insensitive to sharing the fruits of the earth and the work of human hands and while we still allow the barriers of separation and sin to divide us?

But if our unity is lived in the presence of Christ, if we live by his sacrifice, if we live in the company of Christ — and, "catholic" signifies embracing the whole human reality and all persons — then, brothers and sisters, our unity becomes a source of freedom and a message of liberation. It burns with the charity which enlivens and sustains all genuine human solidarity. It does not buckle under the threats of power or become seduced by money. It saves people from being seen as mere particles of nature or engulfed in the anonymity of the secular city. Rather, our unity witnesses to *"a new heaven and a new earth"*, signs of *"liberation which is at hand."*[59]

To Jesus through Mary
(Ad Jesum per Mariam)

I cannot finish, especially in this place, without saying a further word about she who is honoured by this people in the nearby Plaza of the Triumph under the title of the Immaculate Conception. The image of the Immaculate Conception is represented by a wonderful sculpture which Montanés left in this cathedral and which Murillo depicted in his stupendous *Purisima* that was given to the Franciscans of Seville. The tradition of Catholic people has always known how to bind intimately together — without ever placing them in opposition to one another — love for the central mystery of the Eucharist and devotion to the Blessed Virgin Mary. She it is who by her "Fiat" opened the way to the Son's incarnation, which is continued in the mystery of the Church, the body of Christ. She it is who by accompanying her Son to the foot of the Cross is associated with his Sacrifice in sharing with him his redemptive love. She welcomes and accompanies us in her "new motherhood", fruit of the love of the New Covenant. She it is who helps us to live that mystery of communion as God's family, moulding the hearts of sons and brothers and watching over her Son's brothers and sisters along their pilgrim way.

---

[59] Cf. Rev 21:1 ff.

May the Mother of Christ — our Mother, Mother of the Church — help us always to acknowledge, welcome and witness to his Real Presence abiding in our midst, and may she assist us to unite ourselves with his saving Sacrifice and to live the mystery of communion to which we have all been called. Amen.

THE EUCHARISTIC CELEBRATION SUMMIT OF EVANGELIZATION

Cardinal Carlo Maria Martini
Archbishop of Milan

Introduction

The *Church* sprung "from the side of Christ while he slept on the cross"[1] is as it were "a sign and instrument of intimate union with God and of unity among all mankind[2]. The *sacred liturgy* pertains to the Church's essential reality as regards both what constitutes its existence and also what creates its mission.

The liturgy, although "not exhausting the whole action of the Church"[3], can be called "the *summit* towards which the Church's activity tends and, at the same time, the *source* from which flows all its strength."[4] Since it expresses the priestly action of Christ, which it makes real and visible through the priestly action of the Church by the power of the Holy Spirit, the liturgy "achieves its greatest effectiveness in bringing about the sanctification of mankind and the

---

[1] *Sacrosanctum concilium*, no. 5.

[2] *Lumen gentium*, no. 1.

[3] *Sacrosanctum concilium*, no. 9.

[4] *Sacrosanctum concilium*, no. 10.

glorification of God[5]; it thus renews in time the work of divine redemption.

Whatever the Conciliar Constitution (*Sacrosanctum concilium*) states regarding the liturgy in general, applies in a strict and specific way to the *eucharistic celebration*, which is the living heart and nucleus of the sacred liturgy:

> The Eucharist both perfectly signifies and wonderfully effects that communion in God's life and unity of his people, by which the Church exists. It is the summit of both the action by which God sanctifies the world in Christ, and the worship which people offer to Christ and which through him they offer to the Father in the Holy Spirit[6].

Elsewhere we read:

> The celebration of the Mass is the action of Christ and the people of God hierarchically assembled. For both the universal and the local Church, and for each person, it is the centre of the whole Christian life. The Mass reaches the high point of the action by which God in Christ sanctifies the world and the high point of men's worship the Father, as they adore him through Christ, his Son[7].

I have already developed this understanding of the eucharistic mystery in a pastoral context when

---

[5] *Ibid.*

[6] *Eucharisticum mysterium*, no. 6, quoted in the *Catechism of the Catholic Church*, no. 1325.

[7] *General Instruction on the Roman Missal (GIRM)*, ch. I, no. 1 — English tr. in *Instructions on the Revised Roman Rites*, Collins, London, 1979, p. 82.

preparing the Ambrosian Church for the National Eucharistic Congress at Milan in the year 1982-83[8]. At that time, I wrote:

The centrality of the Eucharist must be understood as something utterly unique. It expresses the relation of Jesus with the Father. The Eucharist is a centre of vitality: it gathers us from the fringes of our spiritual exile; it unites us to Jesus in brotherhood and impels us with him and our brothers towards the Father. Like a sun it attracts humanity to itself; it makes mankind together with the world progress towards a mysterious, though sure, goal[9].

In the context of the 45th International Eucharistic Congress I am delighted to take up again this line of thinking, while updating it. Under the overall heading "Eucharist-Evangelization", on which hinges the theme "Christ, Light of the Nations", I restrict myself to dealing with the topic: "the eucharistic celebration, summit of evangelization".

1. Three methodological considerations

In expressing the theme in these terms it seems to me that before tackling the topic it is helpful to state three methodological considerations which I think undergird our entire reflections.

---

[8] Cf. *Attirerò tutti a me: l'Eucaristia al centro della comunità e della sua missione* — "I will draw all to me: the Eucharist at the centre of the community and its mission."

[9] No. 7.

Firstly, regarding the manner of dealing with the topic itself: It is not a question of treating the Eucharist in general terms, but rather on the specific quality of the Eucharist as *celebration* — that is, concerning its liturgical and ritual form in which Christian communities live and celebrate the Eucharist today in the light of the Second Vatican Council and the reforms it introduced. The focus will be, therefore, the actual order of service followed in the celebration of Mass: we shall consider this order as the definitive form of celebrating the Lord's "memorial" and in which the Church shapes its cultic worship in fidelity to Jesus Christ's command to continue in the Church and the world the work of our redemption.

Next, we understand the expression *summit of evangelization*, which is applied to the eucharistic celebration, as implying two distinct yet complementary meanings: on the one hand, the eucharistic celebration (including participation in it) is the *term or climax* towards which the proclamation and welcoming of the Gospel leads; on the other hand, the very dynamic of the eucharistic liturgy celebrates the richest kind of *incentive to evangelization*. The implication of this requires us to point out the reciprocity between all true evangelization leading to the Eucharist and every eucharistic liturgy being an act of evangelisation.

Thirdly, we must be clear about the word "Evangelization". The multiple meanings of this word, which have been examined in the Encyclical Letter *Redemptoris missio* (no. 33) and referred to in the Basic Text of this Congress (no. 7) pertain to *three phases of the Church's nature:* the mission *ad gentes* or strictly missionary evangelization; 2) due pastoral care of the Christian community; 3) the "New Evangelization" or "re-evangelization" of "entire groups of baptized persons who have lost a living sense of faith or do not even regard themselves anymore as members of the Church while leading lives estranged from Christ and his Gospel."[10]

2. Aspects of evangelization pertaining to the eucharistic celebration

The *General Instruction on the Roman Missal* speaks of the structure of the eucharistic celebration as follows:

> Although the Mass is made up of the liturgy of the Word and the liturgy of the Eucharist, the two parts are so closely connected as to form one act of worship. The table of God's word and of Christ's body is prepared and from it the faithful are instructed and nourished. In addition, the Mass has introductory and concluding rites[11].

The Mass, which we daily celebrate for the sanctification of humanity and the glorification of God, consists thus in the twofold table of the Word and the Bread of Life; although the preparatory and concluding rites are secondary, they integrally belong to the whole sweep of the celebration. The universal Church has passed on in its recent liturgical reform what it has culled from the deposit of the rich and time-honoured tradition of faith, which it has finely sifted according to historical, liturgical, theological and

---

[10] *Redemptoris missio*, no. 33.
[11] GIRM, ch. II, no. 8 (English translation, *loc. cit.*, p. 84).

pastoral criteria in order "to bring about conscious, active, and full participation of the people, motivated by faith, hope, and charity."[12]

What is most deeply at stake here is the expression of the sign in the ritual celebration of the Church's fidelity to the Lord's command. As the Fifth Ambrosian Eucharistic Prayer, which is used in the Mass of the Lord's Supper on Maundy Thursday, states: "In obedience to your divine command, Father, we celebrate this mystery." The eucharistic celebration in this way is the radical realization and enduring vital outcome of the work of evangelization which Jesus Christ fulfilled and entrusted to the Apostles and their successors. The Acts of the Apostles speaks of this in the first summary account of the early apostolic community's life: it describes that after hearing the Gospel of Jesus Christ the community "devoted themselves to the apostles' teaching and fellowship, to the breaking of bread and the prayers."[13]

Saint Paul refers to a characteristic element of eucharistic catechesis in writing to the Corinthian Church: "I received from the Lord what I also delivered to you."[14] Finally, we get a glimpse of this in the account of the disciples at Emmaus, where the experience of their Easter faith awakened by the Risen Lord is described in terms of a Sunday eucharistic liturgy: the explanation of the Scriptures along the way; the discernment of the Lord in the breaking of bread and the disciples' mission.

---

[12] *Ibid.*, ch. I, no. 3; Engl. tr., p. 83.

[13] Ac 2:42 — RSV translation.

[14] 1 Cor 11:23.

Insofar as it is recognized as the enduring sign of a community which has received the Gospel (that is, an "evangelized community"), the eucharistic celebration itself furthermore becomes a proclamation of the Gospel addressed to the Church and the world; it is the milieu in which the activity of evangelization is made possible and credible with ceaseless fruitfulness. What are the features of evangelization animating the priceless treasure of the eucharistic liturgy? To what degree, by what means and in what way do our daily and weekly celebrations, which offer us the saving grace of our Lord Christ Jesus himself in his act of paschal self-giving, make available to the community and to every baptized person an effective and fruitful channel of rediscovering and deepening a sense of the Gospel of salvation? To raise these questions does not mean in the slightest that we wish to restrict the task and mission of the Church solely to the eucharistic celebration. Rather, it is a question of gratefully and responsibly recognizing that the sacramental action of the Church's liturgy, which is a popular school of faith, provides an important pedagogical environment of evangelization. The value of this opportunity is missed through hasty, careless and superficial celebrations. While retaining their specific significance the different stages of proclaiming the Gospel can and should lead to an ever fuller and deeper realization of the evangelizing quality of our eucharistic celebration: the first proclamation of the Gospel (*kerygma*), the *lectio divina*, systematic explanation of Christian faith in catechesis and theological study, ecumenical sharing, etc.

I have already referred to the *General Instruction on the Roman Missal* (GIRM no. 8). Now we shall examine in some depth the various elements of this succinct description regarding the Church's celebration of the memorial of the Lord's Passover. We shall see how every eucharistic celebration traces out in its liturgy the path of a wise and well-tried method of evangelization. The steps of this method follow the ecclesiological contexts which have been underlined above.

A. *The introductory rites*

Mass begins with an *ecclesial assembly*, whose ultimate significance is that of a divine assembly. This meaning, however, is not always clear to the minds and hearts of the laity and even, let me say quite frankly, to their pastors. A multitude of various confused motives are mixed with those of faith: an attitude of repeating a ritual action for the sake of religious security and social conformity (i.e. regarding the Mass as an "obligation"; a longing for a place and word that enables one to be cut off from the routine confusion of the rest of the week (i.e. Mass as an "escape" and "pause"); a search for some kind of unusual (exotic) aesthetic or ecstatic experience, which would be psychologically enriching in one way or another (i.e. Mass as a "therapy"). A thousand motives play a part in influencing the attendance of people at Sunday Mass. What should be done? Acknowledge these motives clearly as insufficient and deceptive or, on the contrary, simply accept them without discussion? Obviously the response lies in another approach.

Every approach to celebrate the Eucharist is made up of a mixture of often confused and contradictory *intentions* of the people who are assembled and certain theological, spiritual and ecclesial *requirements*, which relate to the significance of the mystery being celebrated. The Church, in fact, normally suggests to all the faithful, who assemble to celebrate the Lord's Supper, a series of *preparatory rites* in order that their personal intentions become *purified* and that they make their own the *objective reasons* of faith and grace. The opening song, the sign of the cross in the name of the Trinity, the greeting of the assembly by the presiding celebrant, the introductory admonition, the penitential rite with a silent pause, the *gloria* and finally the prayer (the *collect*) — all that makes up the series of the rich and varied gestures and words in the preparatory rites that establish contact, and communication between God and his people and among the people themselves. These rites touch each person at the point of his relationship primarily with God in faith, hope and charity and then to the Church; they invite him to experience the reality of God's meeting with his people through the mediation of Jesus Christ in the power of the Holy Spirit.

It cannot be ever impressed enough upon all the faithful how important it is for them to participate in the whole of the liturgical celebration right from its beginning. There is a vast difference, whether in the communal experience or that of each person, to begin Mass as an assembly already united and prepared or for the most part being gathered in dribs and drabs. In the former situation the introductory rites can exercise their full effectiveness as regards opening the minds and hearts of the faithful to evangelization in the liturgy. In the other, they seem to have no more than a vague and confused sense of marking time till the community is gathered.

B. *The liturgy of the Word*

After it has discovered afresh the theological and ecclesial significance of being gathered as a eucharistic assembly — that is, after it has acknowledged God's mercy towards its sinful condition and raised a hymn of praise and petition to his glory — the community approaches the table of the Word. Here it draws life from the reading of the Scriptures which enable it to encounter the grade of the risen Lord. The liturgy of the Word in its different phases provides a directly *evangilizing* context in the eucharistic celebration. Its contribution to educating the Christian people in faith is enormous, though not always properly appreciated.

The liturgy of the Word *evangelizes* the *act of celebrating,* drawing it into the sweep of the history of salvation, of which it is an actual saving expression rather than having an independent significance. To listen to the Word which is proclaimed in the liturgical assembly offers today — for both the ecclesial community and individuals — the vivid experience of divine revelation, introducing us today to the same school of Jesus, the unique and authentic Teacher, who once taught the people of Israel, the apostolic community and the disciples. The act of proclaiming and explaining the biblical text, which sacramentally realizes the power of the Holy Spirit, transforms the hearing of the words listened to into the vision of what is related[15]. The Second Vatican Council underlined the importance of Christ's real and living presence "already in his Word, through which he speaks when the Church reads the Sacred Scripture."[16]

Furthermore, the liturgy of the Word *evangelizes the approach to the Sacred Scriptures* as regards to the way they are studied, read, meditated or celebrated. For it teaches in a living way how to view the Old and the New Testament as belonging together as a unified whole: prophecy and gospel, psalms and spiritual canticles. The current ordering of the Lectionary and the Christian use of the Hebrew psalter stem from the great insight of the Fathers of the Church, who interpreted the New Testament as prefigured in the Old which it fulfills. The same approach is adopted in the festive celebration of the Word from the first reading to the Gospel: it demonstrates the patient and gradual unfolding of divine revelation and clarifies how the course of the proclamation of the Gospel provides the key to discovering the objective climax of revelation, namely, God's saving dialogue with his people. It can be readily appreciated, therefore, how delicate, beautiful and important is the place of the homily, by means of which a community is led gradually to understand and live the entire wisdom of divine revelation. As I put it in the letter I wrote to the clergy of Milan on Holy Thursday 1983:

> I am reflecting above all on the kind of relationship which exists between the homily and the liturgical action — especially that of the eucharistic celebration

---

[15] Cf. Saint Leo the Great, *Sermo 19 on the Lord's Passion*, Tractatus 70, 1; CCL 138 A, 426.

[16] *Sacrosanctum concilium*, no. 7.

during which it takes place [...] The proclamation made in the homily should help to bring about a transformation of the *listening* to the Word into the *welcoming* of it. In preaching, care must be taken above all to dispose the members of the congregation towards assimilating the Gospel so that they may decide to share in their lives that "logic" which led to Jesus' gift of himself to the Father and for his brethren[17].

In the third place, the liturgy of the word *evangelizes the life of the Christian community* and that of each of the faithful by furthering the holiness of the Church in all respects and at every level. This touches the heart of the evangelizing action of the liturgy of the Word. The proclamation of the Word of God is a way of discerning the "things" of God: it announces consolation and hope for life's pilgrimage; it gives assurance of the availability of grace and salvation always and concerning every human situation in existence; it is an invitation to faith and conversation so that the Church may abound in brotherly charity towards the world; it holds up living examples for imitation and, above all, it succinctly offers an invitation to enjoy already the intimate and transfiguring communion with Jesus Christ as a foretaste of eternal beatitude. The liturgy of the Word does not exhaust the ecclesial and personal attention to it. There are and must be also many other endeavours in the way the Church proclaims, instructs and deepens understanding of the inexhaustible richness of divine revelation, which addresses the ear, penetrates the mind and heart and

---

[17] MARTINI, C.M., *Sia pace sulle tue mura. Discorsi, lettere, omelie (1983-1984)*, Dehoniane, Bologna, 1984, p. 128-129.

renews the life of humanity. Nevertheless, the significance of the Word in the eucharistic liturgy and in other sacramental celebrations remains a necessity for all because of its power to sustain the tension towards sacramental fulness, because of its original capacity to transform listening into a living experience of Christ, because of its unique manner of turning the listening of the divine Scriptures into an event that forms the Church.

Finally, the liturgy of the Word *evangelizes the Church's manner of praying* which it constantly leads back to its genuine biblical inspiration and roots. Once again the prayer of general intercession (or prayer of the faithful) has found its rightful and significant place within the course of the liturgy of the Word. It is not accidentally that this prayer is situated after the biblical readings, after the homily and, on feastdays, after the creed (in the Roman rite). The Church learns and should learn to pray for itself and for the world by listening to the Word of God, for here it welcomes the proclamation of the Father's love for every creature, the love of the Son whose life always intercedes on behalf of those who through him are drawn to God[18], and the gift of the Holy Spirit who "comes to the aid of our weaknesses" and "intercedes for us with sighs too deep for words."[19] The very expression of praise — in the lesser and greater prayers (the collects and eucharistic prayer) which precede, accompany and follow the liturgy of the Word — uncovers in every eucharistic celebration a path to true and real prayer. It can be regarded both

---

[18] Cf. Heb 7:25.
[19] Rm 8:25-26.

as an initiation into the prayer of the Church which has received the Gospel and also as the launching of the praying Church in evangelization[20].

C. *The eucharistic liturgy*

The transition from the liturgy of the Word to that of the Eucharist is an important and delicate step regarding the evangelizing dynamic of the whole eucharistic ritual and of the Christian life which flows from the liturgy. This transition must foster such a deep sense of the exchange and reciprocity between the Word and the Sacrament that enables the faithful to recognize in faith that in fact one has to follow the other: the Word prepares for the Sacrament and the Sacrament realizes the full saving power of the Word.

It is well, above all, to recall how the threefold arrangement of the eucharistic part of the Mass (preparation of the gifts, eucharistic prayer, communion rite) re-enact in a liturgical manner the main *ritual actions of Christ at the Last Supper.* The Church has determined that the unchangeable form of its eucharistic celebration consists in the action of taking bread and wine, that of blessing the one and the other, and the breaking and distribution of these elements after their identity has become substantially something new in virtue of Jesus' words ("This is my body... this is my blood of the covenant")[21]. Even in this part of the celebration — indeed, especially and

---

[20] Cf. in this regard the illuminating work of BIANCHI, E., *Dall'ascolto della Parola alla preghiera liturgica,* Magnano, Qiqajon, 1991.

[21] Mt 26:26-27.

essentially here — the structure of the eucharistic rite is carried out in faithful obedience to the Gospel. In order to become in its own way an unceasing and inexhaustible source of evangelization, the Church's action during the eucharistic liturgy must first of all be exemplary of evangelization. To become the form of the "memorial" of the Lord and of his Passover the Church's action must become the faithful memorial of the ritual actions in which Jesus "on the night when he was betrayed"[22] sacramentally anticipated his entire sacrifice to the Father for the world on the altar of the cross.

Now we shall examine the above-mentioned three parts of the eucharistic liturgy in turn regarding how each of them shares in the dynamic of evangelization: the rites of presenting preparing the gifts; the eucharistic prayer, and the communion rite.

1) *The rites of presenting/preparing the gifts* have become clearer since they were simplified after the Council. Their significance consists in guaranteeing and proclaming in an ever clearer and direct manner the *goodness of creation and its supernatural purpose.* On the one hand, the sacrament, which is taken from material things ("the fruit of the earth and the work of human hands", in the words of the offertory prayers), bears witness to the original goodness of earthly realities and to God's blessing conferred on human endeavour in transforming the world. On the other hand, the radical and unimaginable newness of what becomes of these material things — namely, to be the sacrament of Jesus' Body and Blood — calls into

---

[22] 1 Cor 11:23.

question every merely materialistic kind of endeavour, which is incapable of awakening humanity to the mystery of God and to receiving the gift of a new "supersubstantial" and "heavenly" bread[23]. There are many implications which flow from this manner of regarding the preparation of the gifts for the task of evangelizing our contemporary Western culture; to find again a new capacity to offer praise (blessing) when viewing created realities and human work; to rediscover a sense of God's providence throughout creation; to create space for gratitude and appreciation of the transcendant aspect permeating daily life.

2) *The Eucharistic Prayer,* which is the centre and heart of every Mass, would merit treatment on its own in another conference because it is so rich in implications regarding the essential focus of the Church's mission to proclaim the Gospel. I am going to treat only two aspects from among such a vast range of possible approaches: *i)* the basic twofold rhythm of its structure[24]; and *ii)* the emphasis placed on the dynamic or pneumatological dimension of the

---

[23] Cf. Mt 6:11 — Cf. the eucharistic reinterpretation which the liturgy and Fathers give of the request in the Lord's Prayer for bread; cf. also Jn 6:51.

[24] Which has been so well uncovered in the recent studies of Fr Cesare Giraudo — cf. *La struttura letteraria della preghiera eucaristica. Saggio sulla genesi letteraria di una forma. Torah veterotestamentaria, Berakah giudaica, Anafora cristiana,* Analecta biblica 92, Roma, Biblical Institute Press, 1981; *Eucaristia per la Chiesa. Prospettive teologiche sull'Eucaristia a partire dalla "lex orandi",* Aloisiana 22, Roma-Brescia, Gregoriana-Morcelliana, 1989; *Preghiere eucaristiche per la Chiesa di oggi. Riflessione in margine al commento del canone svizzero-romano,* Aloisiana 23, Brescia-Roma, Morcelliana-Gregorian University Press, 1993.

whole eucharistic mystery, especially in the new texts of the recent liturgical reforms.

i) The structure of the eucharistic prayer, which is derived from the Old Testament *torah* and Jewish *berakah*, is presented both as an *anamnesis*, that is the *memorial celebration of God's deeds*, and also as an *epiclesis*, that is the calling upon the power of God to bring about salvation, which is truly realized through the sacrament. The eucharistic prayer resounds in utter harmony with biblical revelation of God's saving deeds in history insofar as it begins with thanksgiving, praise, celebration, exaltation of God and his saving involvement in the human condition. At the climax of recalling God's great deeds done "for us men and for our salvation"[25] the Church remembers his Son, Jesus Christ and his Passover, which is the event and sacrament he left as "the everlasting sign of your covenant."[26] The emphasis is shifted in the prayer of "epiclesis" (or invocation) that follows — either explicitly of implicitly — from the attitude of recalling to that of asking God to send the Spirit to realize or bring about what is remembered with gratitude and praise:

And so, Father, we bring you these gifts. We ask you to make them holy by the power of your Spirit, that they may become the body and blood of your Son, our Lord Jesus Christ, at whose command we celebrate this eucharist[27].

---

[25] Cf. the Nicean-Constantinopolitan Creed.

[26] *Eucharistic Prayer for Reconciliation I* — ICEL translation.

[27] *Eucharistic Prayer III* — ICEL translation.

The real and substantial presence of Christ in the sacramental signs of bread and wine, which sacramentally re-presents the sacrifice of the cross, enables us to become truly united to Christ in building up his Church. This presence is the adorable fruit of "the sacrifice of praise and supplication" with which the Church blesses the bread and wine in faithful obedience to the Lord's command.

Our people are insufficiently aware of this matter. For the most part the attention of the faithful is focused too often merely on the words of institution and the double elevation rather than on the prayerful context of praise and supplication through which the eucharistic elements are consecrated. Above all else it is our responsibility, as bishops and priests, to bring about a deeper awareness of the theological and spiritual significance of the different parts and their overall unity in the way in which we carry out the words and ritual gestures of the eucharistic or consecratory prayer entrusted to us in a special way. There is nothing against, rather it is highly recommended, to explain the richness of the texts of the eucharistic prayer in relation to their catechetical or mystagogical significance and to the reality of the Eucharist.

ii) The theological and spiritual dynamic of the eucharistic prayer is the other specific dimension that merits to be rediscovered. The bread and wine become the Body and Blood of Jesus Christ by the action of the Holy Spirit *in order that* all who eat this bread and drink the chalice may "be filled with his Holy Spirit, and become one body, one spirit in Christ."[28] The Church's ritual celebration is presided over by

---

[28] *Eucharistic Prayer III* — ICEL translation.

the priest and the whole assembly of the faithful participates in it by the power of the Holy Spirit. Here the Church offers itself and the world, the eucharistic and sacramental Body of the Lord Jesus so that in the communion banquet of the one Bread, all of us may become his mystical and ecclesial Body, his holy people, his Church. The development of the themes of the different eucharistic prayers from the past and today, always point to the ecclesial outcome of every Eucharist: *the real specific fruit of the Mass consists in the building of the Christian community in a communion of life — like that of a marriage — with Jesus Christ* and, as flowing from this, *a sharing of the final end of one's brethren in faith.* In the practice of adoration and contemplation of the Blessed Sacrament, which is signified in the double elevation and which takes place in the different forms of eucharistic worhsip outside Mass, we must never lose sight of this primary purpose of the sacrament; thus, it is in this ecclesial rather than individual perspective that we must continually seek to renew eucharistic devotions.

iii) The communion rite takes up and realizes the Christological and ecclesial orientation of the eucharistic banquet — just as in the eucharistic prayer, which in its turn remains faithful to the eucharistic catechesis contained in the New Testament. The Eucharist is first and foremost the daily *bread* — the bread of wayfarers and the nourishment necessary to fulfil every stage of life's journeying and calling. By being nourished with this bread every baptized person becomes drawn ever more deeply into *the meaning of the life of Him who offers himself as food:* he learns to think, act and love according to the standards revealed by the Spirit of Christ; he grows to enjoy living as a child of God, wholly obedient to the Father's will; he receives as a gift the sure pledge of eternal life which Jesus promised at Capernaum: "he who eats my flesh and drinks my blood has eternal life, and I will raise him up at the last day."[29] The Eucharist creates at the same time and in a complementary way *the experience of a new brotherhood;* it enables us to become attentive, dedicated, responsible and forgiving. All the rites which surround the reception of Holy Communion signifiy the reality of the Gospel of love and foster its practice in living: the communal procession towards the sacrament, the extension of one's hand in an act of begging for the same Bread of life, the *amen* which bears witness in a personal way to the Church's one faith, the communion song in unison with all one's brethren and the communal silence of deep gratitude.

Thus, in the transition from the offering preparation of the gifts to the communion rite by the necessary step of the eucharistic prayer, the eucharistic liturgy evangelizes the Church and the world to receive in Jesus Christ God's last and definitive gift to humanity; it manifests that in communion with him a realistic way becomes available to all for the building of a new humanity of unity and brotherhood. As I put it in my book *Attirerò a me:*

> Especially through the eucharistic celebration a Christian learns to imitate the charity of Jesus [...] and recognizes that his own capability of offering himself to the Father has its roots in the offering which Christ made of his entire self[30].

---

[29] Jn 6:54.

[30] *Loc. cit.*, no. 7-71.

D. *The concluding rites*

The Mass ends by turning the congregation towards its mission of living out what it has celebrated. The prayer after communion asks that the Eucharist may be fruitful in producing moral, spiritual and eschatological effects in the participants, who are entrusted with the task of making these effects evident and of revealing to the world the new face of humanity, that of the Lord's disciples[31]. The blessing in the name of the Holy Trinity, which precedes and prepares for the final dismissal of the congregation, summarizes in a significant way the richness of God's gifts which have been savoured during the eucharistic celebration; it offers these gifts as a viaticum which the congregation witnesses and communicates to the world. Finally, the formula of dismissal ("The Mass is ended. Go in peace") expresses at one and the same time both an invitation to look after the gift received and also a challenge to live the Church's mission:

When the community does not focus on its own plans or its own structures or its own needs, but on Jesus present in the Eucharist, its objective *missionary identity* becomes clear as directed to every person, every situation, every human environment to which the joyful proclamation of Christ's Passover must be addressed and which must become involved in celebrating God's love[32].

---

[31] Cf. Mt 7:16-20.
[32] *Attirerò tutti a me*, no. 73.

3. What is required to bring out the riches of the eucharistic celebration for evangelization

When in fidelity to the Lord's command due attention is paid to the unfolding of the word and the ritual actions in the eucharistic celebration, it becomes clear that the structure of the liturgy fosters the Church's task of evangelization. In its own way and according to its particular characteristics the eucharistic celebration, which itself issues from the evangelizing action of Christ and the Church, offers each Christian community, taken as it is, a mixture of faith and disbelief, and also every believer the opportunity to experience grace and salvation. Because this experience comprises both tangible signs *(per signa sensibilia)* and a means of passing from the Word to the Sacrament to communion (with Christ and, through him with the Father and our brethern), it embodies the formative power of the liturgy for proclamation, witness and mission.

It is here that there arises the serious and urgent matter of making the transition from liturgical objectives to their realization in the living experience of our communities. What is required to "liberate" the potential for evangelization of our eucharistic celebration? What kind of liturgical and pastoral stimulus is needed to empower the eucharistic assemblies of our Churches to become truly evangelical? I maintain that the positive and adequate answer to these questions lies in *liturgical education*.

The Holy Father wrote at the beginning of his pontificate: "What is needed [...] and urgently appropriate is to undertake again a true *education* in order to discover the riches contained in the liturgy."[33] These words of Pope John Paul II do not appear to be superfluous today; rather they deserve to be taken to heart at this 45th International Eucharistic Congress. Concern about liturgical education continues to decline in many "pastoral strategies" of the '80s and '90s, and one has the impression that there is confusion in facing the Church's role in regard to ritual celebration. This confusion hinders the development of a careful and systematic education of the Christian community to lead the faithful to an intelligent, pious and active participation in the signs, words and liturgical rites of the mystery celebrated. I am not going to tackle here the question of the "on-going liturgical formation" of the clergy and the liturgical training of future priests and deacons in seminaries and of students for religious life — topics that are presupposed and indispensable in what follows[34]. Instead I shall speak about the liturgical education of the faithful who attend our Sunday Masses either occasionally or out of habit.

A. *Education in the language of celebration*

Firstly, we must underline the need for a periodic and regular education in the different kind of language employed in the liturgy — biblical, laudatory, ritual, symbolic, gesture, "iconic", etc.

* This education should be provided *before* the eucharistic celebration. We should avoid where possible unnecessary meetings and courses, but make the

---

[33] In the letter *Dominicæ cenæ* (1980), no. 9.
[34] The topics might be dealt with later in a study-group.

best of the many opportunities which are already available for proclamation and catechesis in which the education of a community of faith is expressed. Gospel discussions, "schools of the Word", adult catechesis, youth formation, instruction of children and teenagers geared to round off their Christian initiation, special themes treated in preaching, etc., all these forms of evangelization should enable a deepening of the significance of a liturgical-sacramental life both at theological and spiritual levels and also at the practical level of experience. Among so many opportunities for liturgical catechesis particular care should be taken over that which prepares children for their First Holy Communion. For they should learn on this occasion the ABC of Christianity and, particularly, its liturgical and sacramental language.

* Education also must be provided *within* the eucharistic celebration by taking care to make the best of all its aspects — words, song, gesture, silence, ministries involved, manner of presiding and conducting the liturgy, etc. This does not mean that teaching on these aspects is introduced during the Mass, but that the manner of realizing these various aspects during the time available becomes effective in communicating the significance of the salvific event celebrated in the sacred rites. As I said to the people of my diocese in 1990:

Rather than going into complicated explanations and using difficult terminology, it is worthwhile to seek ways of rediscovering those expressions which stimulate faith, whether verbal or non-verbal. These well-tried means have always occupied an important place in Christian tradition, although in recent times they have not always been appreciated enough because of a lack of understanding of their importance.[35]

To realize this task of enlivening the liturgy requires preparation and competent handling, humility and dedication, a sense of faith and profound appreciation of the Church's tradition.

* Finally, this education is *followed up after* the eucharistic celebration in linking the various forms of popular devotion and personal spirituality of the faithful ever more closely and explicitly with the celebration of the Eucharist. In this regard, it is worthwhile to highlight the endeavours of parishes and groups to rediscover the place of Morning and Evening Prayer as that communal prayer which is the twofold pivot of divine worship. For their intrinsic value lies in forming a sense of praying with the word of God, principally the use of the psalms.

B. *Education in participation*

In the second place we must pay careful attention to what fosters a mature and comprehensive approach regarding *cooperation in ministry*. On this topic we should take up again in our communities the entire chapter dealing with participation of the faithful in the eucharisitic celebration in order thay they may share intimately and fully in the grace of the mystery they celebrate. The *General Instruction on the Roman Missal* states:

---

[35] MARTINI, C.M., *Effatà, apriti. Lettera per il programma pastorale "comunicare"*, Milano, 1990/92.

It is of the highest importance that the celebration of Mass or the Lord's Supper be carried out in such a way that the ministers and faithful, who share in it according to their proper function and state, draw those abundant fruits which Christ the Lord intended to bestow in instituting the eucharistic sacrifice of his Body and Blood and which he entrusted to the Church, his beloved Bride as a memorial of his passion and resurrection.[36]

Many strides ahead have been made in these recent years. We can undoubtedly rejoice in the signs of ecclesial vitality, among which are the following: the care for the breadth of ministry exercised in our celebration (choral expression of the responses, prayers, ritual gestures, etc.); exercise of lay ministries (in proclaiming the Word of God, service at the altar, distribution of communion by special ministers, leading of the song and music, ministry of welcome, preparation of texts, care of the sacristy and arrangement of the sanctuary, etc.).

However, I would like to touch upon an aspect of "participation" which still remains unsatisfactorily treated. It is unfortunately not new to hear the complaint that, whereas the liturgical reform has brought about an intelligent, active and external participation of the assembly, there has been scant attention given to the significance of a more *interior and spiritual* participation — viz. participation that is full, interior, fervent in faith, hope and charity, as envisaged in the General Instruction[37]. The emphasis on "doing" or "carrying out" the ritual celebration has (and does)

---

[36] GIRM, no. 2.
[37] *Ibid.*, no. 3

run the risk of depriving our eucharistic liturgies — and hence the life and faith of our people — of their contemplative and prayerful spirit. In a provocative, through wholly honest way the theologian von Balthasar put it like this:

> Where are the worship and adoration in our up to date services? Thinking either that these functions are superfluous or that churchgoers aren't mature enough, the clergy have taken it into their heads to fill out the time in a practical way and with a pretty varied run of activities: there's not a moment left free. Noisy all the time; if it's not prayers out loud or Bible readings and expositions, then it's singing and responses that have to be listened to...[38]

In order that we re-establish a correct and needed balance between action and contemplation, we must rediscover in a committed and creative way how to integrate into the various ministries of the word, gesture, song, etc. the ministry of silence — that silence of knowing how to remain in the presence of the Lord; that silence of listening and meditating the Word; that silence of prayer through which the attention of the person praying becomes gradually attuned to the words employed. The time devoted to preparation before Mass, the use of silence at moments during the celebration of liturgy, personal thanksgiving after Mass, the renewal of the different kinds of communal and personal eucharistic worship... all these are but aspects of the overall significance of living the liturgy.

---

[38] VON BALTHASAR, H.U., *Who is a Christian?*, (translated by John Cumming, Burns & Oates, A Compass Book, London, 1968, p. 34).

The fostering of this life requires great care especially today so that those who celebrate the Eucharist may be evangelized and by their living and sharing the Mass they may be impelled in their turn to become evangelizers.

Adoration and contemplative silence are not something added to the eucharistic celebration, but are nourished by it and express its deepest reality. Adoration of the mystery of God "in spirit and truth" (Jn 4:24) leads to living the meaning of the eucharistic celebration; and insofar as the celebration is meant to draw the whole of life by the vitality of Jesus and his Spirit into the mystery of the Father, it leads to adoration[39].

4. Conclusions

We are now in a position to point out briefly three ways of testing the meaning and particular vitalizing evergy of the Eucharist for Christian living. These concerns are: 1) the community formed by the Eucharist; 2) the Eucharist and catechesis; and, 3) the Eucharist and the service of charity.

A. *The community formed by the Eucharist*

While caracterizing and unifying the community's tasks, gestures and endeavours, the Eucharist above all has a profound effect on its spiritual life, that is, its influence is evident in the ways in which the Holy

---

[39] MARTINI, C.M., *Attirerò tutti a me*, p. 88-89.

Spirit brings the lives of individual persons and their interpersonal relations with one another into conformity with Jesus' pattern of living. It is important, therefore, that every Christian community examine itself regarding the spiritual qualities it should derive from celebrating the Eucharist. Every community — parish, group, diocese — should find in the Eucharist the needed spiritual resources to tackle the concrete problems arising occasionally in its life. Thus, in times of tension or division it offers us the spirit of peace. In times of confusion and obscurity it challenges us to become refreshed through prayer. In facing difficulties or calamities it strengthens our sense of solidarity. When so many immigrants seek hospitality and integration into our midst it shows us how to be welcoming. On occasions of bereavement, discouragement and spiritual weakness it awakens hope, etc. In each case, the Eucharist is the bond that binds together the whole life of the Church with all the situations of need confronting it.

This creative attitude is fully realized in the local Church or diocese. It is also experienced in that local community which is the parish. The eucharistic celebration provides the privileged, though not exclusive, context of this regenerative tension. Furthermore, the parish is the privileged, though not exclusive, environment through which the Eucharist gathers, forms and unifies the concrete expressions of the Church's life.

B. *The Eucharist and catechesis*

One of the fundamental tasks of the Christian community consists in proclaiming and listening to the Word. Catechesis is one aspect of this task. When catechesis is related to the Eucharist, which draws all life together in Christ, it follows that the Word also calls every person to be in communion with Jesus' Passover. Consequently, in the light of the Eucharist, catechesis must be related to and embrace every stage of living. In fact, the influence of the Eucharist on humanity is not something piece meal or fragmentary, but brings about a thorough-going integration of the different moments in the development of human existence.

Furthermore, in the light of the Eucharist, catechesis is undertaken in such a way that it carefully permeates the rhythm of the liturgical year and becomes integrated into the *lectio divina*. By means of the *lectio divina* the deep transforming effect of the Eucharist of the whole of human life becomes even more relevant and personal.

Finally, the limitations of catechetical endeavours become apparent when they are renewed in the context of the Eucharist, which is the supreme gesture of Christ's love for every person; thus, instead of being an abstract and merely didactic exercise, they become charged with the power to communicate that love imbued with humility which ever seeks new ways of reaching out even to people who are far off and confused.

C. *The Eucharist and the service of charity*

The Eucharist means that charity is the teaching of those who have allowed themselves to be drawn by Jesus. Before it is a "good work" or an action, charity is a spiritual environment that unites the community in the singlemindedness of mercy.

The Eucharist tells us also about the horizon towards which the service of charity is oriented. In the paschal mystery the love of Jesus was unfolded in the context of his courageous acceptance of death, defeat and human wickedness — that context which leads to the resurrection.

The charity which Christians receive from the Eucharist has these qualities. While it challenges us not to shirk suffering, it assures us that the final victory over evil is something that the world cannot give, a gift coming directly from the heart of the Father. For whoever imagines that an immediate and completely satisfactory solution can be found by facing the problem of evil by his own efforts is doomed to the dangers of self-delusion. Christians, on the other hand, receive from the love shown in the Eucharist a message of hope so that not even the danger of defeat can crush them.

In the third place, the Eucharist points to those who are the special focus of charity — namely, those whom Jesus loved most of all. Charity which takes its shape from the Eucharist seeks every person who is suffering — the sick, the outcast, the drug-addict, the refugee, the prisoner. To these the presence of Christ is proclaimed in order to reveal to them that, even in their condition, the seed of love can take root and to assure them that if they can only believe in love and live from love they have found salvation.

The Eucharist brings about the Kingdom in the world not by mere human effort, but through the powerful action of the Spirit of the risen Lord. To put the Eucharist at the centre means acknowledging its formative power, being disposed to allow it to work in us not only as individuals, but also as a Christian community, and surrendering ourselves to the challenges and implications of this unique and revolutionary event which is Christ's Passover inserted into human history.

In rediscovering that the eucharistic event is the centre of the whole Church's development, we shall discover thus the fullest significance of this Eucharistic Congress.

THE EVANGELIZING RICHES
OF THE EUCHARIST

Anthony McSweeney, s.s.s.
Former Superior General of the
Congregation of the Blessed Sacrament

*"You are proclaiming the death of the Lord
until he comes"*

Introduction

As the two disciples trudged disconsolately towards the village of Emmaus, they listened to the
stranger with growing fascination. Long familiar
words of the Scriptures took on new meaning, dashed
hopes began to revive. A mysterious transformation
was taking place within them, though they did not yet
notice it. Only later, seated at table would they become aware of what was taking place. Jesus "took the
bread and said the blessing; then he broke it and
handed it to them. And their eyes were opened and
they recognized him."[1]

---

[1] Lk 24:30-31.

The story is universally recognized as referring to the Church's Eucharistic experience. It can lead us into our theme: *the evangelizing riches of the Eucharist.*

The image of the Eucharist which emerges from this story is that of the presence of the risen Lord to his own. He, the Christ who died, rose and is to come, the definitive word of salvation, is seated with his diciples at the table. Present sacramentally to his disciples, he is the fulfillment of all the words of the Scriptures, which are summed up in the paschal proclamation. This is the central message, the core of the Church's proclamation of faith, its *kerygma*. The whole of Jesus' life as incarnation of the Word converges on it.

This kerygma is announced in a unique way in the Eucharist. There it finds its summit, its fullest realization.

The Eucharist as proclamation

The *evangelizing* character of the Eucharist is not something secondary or added to it. It belongs to the very nature of the celebration of the Sacrament. We believers who repeat these words and deeds *"in memory"* of Jesus proclaim thereby his saving death as the source of meaning and hope for our own lives. We proclaim the kingdom in the face of all that might seem to engulf and destroy God's good world in our own history and in our own lives.

We do this, moreover, not just for ourselves, but as *"priestly people"*. We stand before God and bless and praise his name, re-enacting the Supper in an act of faith in the mystery which is for all peoples, in all places and in all times. We proclaim in this act that Jesus is the Lord, that in his death we are freed from the power of death and from the fear it awakens in us[2], that we are set free from the hold of sin, which works through death, and that we are made capable of love. That is *"good news"* indeed!

Although the mystery which it proclaims concerns every human being, the evangelizing power of the Eucharist is aimed at the community of believers as such. The celebration, therefore, constitutes the *"summit"* of the Church's self-evangelization, in order to become, in turn, the *"source"* of its evangelizing mission towards the world[3].

We can explore our theme by thinking of the Eucharist as an act of *proclamation.* It is this which Paul intended when he wrote to the Corinthians, "Whenever you eat this bread, then, and drink this cup, you are proclaiming the death of the Lord until he comes."[4]

1. Proclaiming the death of the Lord

As well as being the great act in which the Christian community proclaims and participates in its salvation, the Eucharist, as reserved Sacrament, has become a source of spiritual nourishment for many believers over the centuries through the practice of Eucharistic adoration. I shall, therefore, look at the evangelizing riches of the Eucharist both as sacramen-

---

[2] Cf. Heb 2:14-15.

[3] Cf. *Sacrosanctum concilium,* no. 10; *Lumen gentium,* no. 11; *Presbyterorum ordinis,* no. 5.

[4] 1 Cor 11:26.

tal celebration and as adoration of the reserved Sacrament.

A. *In the celebration of the Eucharist*

When the community gathered *"in his name"* celebrates the Supper *"in memory"* of Jesus, it proclaims its faith in Jesus' own interpretation of his death, namely as the event through which, according to God's provident love, the definitive and long-awaited divine *kingdom* would become powerful operative in the world. The community attests its belief that this salvation, which was made manifest in the resurrection of Jesus and experienced as transforming power in the outpouring of the Spirit, now opens our human future towards a radically new dimension of fulfillment.

The liturgical reform has given this character of proclamation a verbal form through the acclamation by which the gathered people respond to the institution narrative: *"Christ has died, Christ is risen, Christ will come again!"* The Eucharist is already a proclamation, however, in a much more comprehensive sense, as I have suggested.

The Eucharist evangelizes, is a proclamation of the Gospel, through the rite which embodies the kerygma, through the liturgy of the Word and, in some degree at least, in the behaviour of the celebrating community[5]. We shall look briefly at each of these aspects.

[5] Cf. BIERITZ, K.-H., "Structures de l'annonce", *La Maison-Dieu*, no. 154, 1983, p. 37-57.

The rite as proclamation

Everything takes place around a table. It is here, says Hans Urs Von Balthasar, that our approach to the Eucharist must start.

> The accent must fall on the encounter of Christ and the Church in the act of the meal: this is where the centre of gravity lies [...] The true sacramental sign in the Eucharist is the event of eating and drinking[6].

Already the symbolism of table-fellowship is rich with meaning. One of the earliest expressions for the Eucharist, *the breaking of bread,* draws upon this fund of meaning.

Just as the sharing of bread and wine, received with a blessing as a gift to be shared, represented the participation in God's gift of life, so Jesus' offer to share his own body and blood with us in the gesture of offering bread and wine revealed his understanding of his own life as a gift received from the Father in gratitude, to be given back to him through being shared as nourishment with his *friends*[7]. His table thereby became God's table at which, through him, human beings were called to sit in fellowship and reconciliation.

The eucharistic prayer enshrines and explicitates this proclamation. The content of the Supper is Jesus' life as such and its significance, summed up in the Paschal Mystery. The gesture of giving, in grateful

---

[6] VON BALTHASAR, H.U., *The Glory of the Lord. A Theological Aesthetics,* Vol. 1, Crossroad, New York, 1982, p. 573.

[7] Cf. Jn 15:14-15.

response for the gift of life, constitutes that life's epitome.

Each part of the celebratory rite unfolds a dimension of the essential Mystery. It evangelizes in leading the participants through a series of actions — of assembling, of signing themselves in faith, repenting, listening, confessing faith, praising, thanking, praying, sharing, declaring peace, and so on[8]. In the rite, deeds and words are inseparately united. Jesus' act of sharing food and drink at the Last Supper as a sign of his own self-giving is not simply a picture or illustration; it is a language which stands on its own and as such is not reducible to words. It is a "visible word" in its own right, like the acts performed by the prophets of old.

Proclamation by the Word

Just as in the Emmaus episode, the liturgy of the Word, which prepares the eucharistic prayer, is also intended to proclaim salvation by means of the hearing of the Scriptures. The words and deeds of Jesus are recalled and meditated in the context of the whole of the Scriptures.

The readings are a saving Word which is offered to the assembly as God's present. It is the function of the homily to enable the congregation to hear that Word as addressed to it in its own actual experience. The homily is a form of discourse that takes its character also from its Eucharistic context. Saint Peter Julian Eymard, for example, liked to prepare his homilies in the presence of the Eucharistic bread. He said that he

---

[8] See the Congress preparatory Basic Text no. 14.

meditated the Word in presence of the Sacrament so that, exposed *to the Eucharistic fire*, it might become tasty and substantial bread. *"I make the dough"*, he said picturesquely, *"and it cooks in the Eucharistic oven."*

The Scriptural words are present throughout the celebration, however. One especially potent moment is the recitation of the Lord's prayer. I have been struck by the stories certain people have told me of powerful experiences of conversion which have occurred at the moment of reciting this prayer. In its Eucharistic setting the Word seems to unleash its power in a special way.

The liturgical proclamation, however, is far from exhausting the evangelizing dimension of the Eucharist. The celebration evangelizes in other ways as well. Paul refers to the eating and drinking as having the character of proclaiming the death of the Lord. In what way is this so?

The community which accepts to gather *"in memory"* of him, and repeats in the power of the Spirit his gesture, makes that life and the gestures which epitomizes it its own. It proclaims it as the decisive event of human history. It actually enters into the enactment, accepting the offer of bread and cup and eating and drinking what the Lord offers it. By so doing the participants make an act of personal commitment, undertaking to reproduce in their own lives the attitude of self-giving embodied in the Eucharistic gesture.

We are, therefore, on the threshold of a further dimension of the proclamatory character of the Eucharist. For the verbal and ritual declarations we make in celebrating the Eucharist together cannot be separated from the way we actually live.

What our deeds proclaim

It was this link between celebration and life that Paul wanted the Corinthians to see. For the way they were treating one another was in flagrant contradiction with the meaning that they were proclaiming and enacting in their celebration of the Lord's Supper. Effectively, he tells them, their behaviour annulled the Supper. He was very forthright. The community gatherings, he declared, were *"doing more harm than good"*[9]; indeed, he says quite bluntly, *"it is not the Lord's Supper that you eat."*[10] What in fact they are proclaiming is not their salvation from the power of evil over their lives. On the contrary, they are announcing their own condemnation. As a result of their selfish behaviour, the Supper has become for them a source of death rather than of life.

It is very clear then that the day to day behaviour of the community enters into the proclamatory character of its Eucharistic celebration. Christian liturgy cannot abstract from actual life, which in fact constitutes a critical criterion of the authenticity of the community's worship. Unless we celebrate in the truth, we do not celebrate at all, in the sense that we enact a lie, which empties our celebration of its essential meaning. *"It is not the Lords' Supper that you eat"*. For the liturgy proclaims present power, nor a theory or a mere ideal; the proclamation of this power is emptied of its force or contradicted if we cannot see any signs of its work in the community which celebrates.

---

[9] 1 Cor 11:17.
[10] 1 Cor 11:20.

Conditions of proclamation

The Eucharistic liturgy should not be considered in isolation from its wider contexts. For although it always retains its intrinsic power, thanks to the Lord's promise, it does normally rely upon various forms of mediation to achieve its goal. As the *"summit"* of the evangelizing process, it presupposes initiation and the support of Christian formation. Deprived of these, as the *Basic Text* obverves[11], the liturgy is impoverished and its transforming power bridled.

What I have been saying thus far may be difficult to connect at times with the average Sunday experience of many people precisely because the liturgy is so often badly celebrated. As our society becomes secularized[12], many baptized persons are finding liturgy boring and meaningless and are ceasing to practice. Of course, the Lord is free to touch hearts as he will, but the liturgical form through which the evangelizing riches of the Supper are intended to act upon the participants must normally be allowed to speak its unique word as effectively as possible. Liturgical renewal, therefore, must remain a constant priority for the Church as condition for the effectiveness of the Sacrament as proclamation of the Mystery of Christ.

---

[11] See no. 12.

[12] Not in the sense that the sacred is disappearing from society; but that it is taking new forms, often outside the familiar contexts of religion, as a number of writers have pointed out in re-assessing the concept of secularization. See, for example, John Coleman, "The Situation for Modern Faith", *Theological Studies*, vol. 39, no. 4, Dec. 1978, p. 601-632; Paul Valadier, "L'Église en procès", *Catholicisme et société moderne*, Flammarion, 1989, p. 17-60.

The evangelizing character of the Eucharist, then, pervades the celebration and operates in word, through the prayers and responses, the Scripture readings and the homily; it is a proclamation also in the very ritual gestures themselves, as well as in the concrete behaviour of the community, especially as reflected in its social relations.

B. *In the forms of Eucharistic adoration*

The concern behind the renewal promoted by Vatican II to restore the liturgy to its central place in the life of the Church has brought out more clearly the relative character of the centuries-old practice of Eucharistic adoration in relation to the liturgical celebration of the mystery. Above all, adoration is seen as *"prolonging the grace of the sacrifice"* and particularly of sacramental communion[13]. Whether in a public form, with prolonged or briefer periods of exposition, or in a private form of personal devotion, Eucharistic adoration has as its purpose the recognition of the sacramental presence of the risen Christ who gives himself to his people as their *"bread of life"* and the fostering of a deeper communion with him.

Though it is not a sacramental act in itself[14], Eucharistic adoration is never to be conceived of outside the

---

[13] Cf. *Eucharisticum mysterium*, nos. 3, 49, 50; John Paul II, *Dominicæ cœnæ*.

[14] The various forms of Eucharistic adoration belong to the order of prayer and devotion rather than to that of sacramental action as such, and hence do not partake of the efficacy proper to the sacramental order.

sacramental frame of reference proper to the liturgical celebration of the Eucharist. Its nature and content are entirely determined by the way the Church understands the celebration; its value, in fact, lies in its preparing us to participate with more awareness in the liturgy and in deepening our union with Christ given in sacramental communion. Prayer and devotions directed to Christ in the sacramental species will open us to the evangelizing riches of the Eucharist to the degree to which they respect the movement and the finality of the celebration, namely worship of the Father through Jesus Christ in the Holy Spirit, and deeper union with Christ in his Paschal Mystery.

Eucharistic adoration is a precious mean of deepening in the faithful the fundamental attitudes of faith, gratitude and praise, offering, universal prayer and adoring love which are the very heart of all Eucharistic worship. According to the post-Vatican II guidelines, such devotions are to reflect the communitarian character of salvation and to be illuminated (according to the liturgical season) by the Word of God, inseparable from the Eucharist, and must lead to Christian witness in personal and social life.

The loving communion with Christ, sacramentally present, which has always been the living heart of Eucharistic devotion, must be developed in full respect for the sacramental signs which the Lord himself has chosen as vehicles for this mystery; and these must be understood, furthermore, in their full liturgical context[15]. If Eucharistic devotion has been looked

---

[15] Care needs to be taken lest the riches of theses signs be reduced by isolating the consecrated bread, whether exposed in the monstrance or reserved in the tabernacle, from its fuller context which includes, amongst others, the sign of the commu-

upon sometimes with suspicion, this has been due to misplaced accents[16] based on a vision of the sacramental presence virtually separated from the full dimensions of the Eucharistic action. The forms of prayer used, whilst adapted to a more meditative context, should be in harmony with the liturgy. Adoration offers a precious opportunity for getting to know, in a prayerful and meditative ways, the *anaphoras* of Eucharistic prayers, for example. Still too little understood by Christians, they are a rich resource for prayer and teach us that the first form of evangelization is the confession of God's saving presence in our world, such as we find in Jesus' own *"hymn of jubilation"*[17] and in a striking way in Mary's *Magnificat*.

It seems to me that, understood in this way, Eucharistic adoration offers us a splendid opportunity for promoting a more personalized awareness of the riches of the mystery of Christ contained in the Eucharist, above all in regard to the profound union with Christ and his members which is fruit of the Sacrament. Thus the testimony of life which results will have greater evangelizing impact inasmuch as it arises out of a more deeply interiorized experience.

---

nity gathered about the Lord's table as well as the initial gestures and words (cf. *Eucharisticum mysterium*, nos. 4, 60-62, 63-65.

[16] Forgetting that the Christ present through the Eucharistic species is the glorious Christ, who nourishes his people with a view to incorporating them into his Paschal Mystery, certain rather widespread devotions have given an excessive emphasis to aspects such as reparation, based at times on an inaccurate vision of Christ as abandoned, ever imprisoned in the sacramental state and needing to be visited and consoled. For want of adequate formation, the current revival of Eucharistic devotions is not always free of such regressive tendencies.

[17] Cf. Mt 11:25-27; Lk 10:21-22.

Thus far we have looked at the way in which the evangelizing riches of the Eucharist are present in the liturgical celebration and how they can be assimilated through the various forms of Eucharistic adoration directed to Christ present in the reserved Sacrament. It is now time to reflect upon these riches themselves which, evangelizing the community, are intended to fashion it into an effective evangelizing people. We can take as our point of departure the power of the Eucharist to introduce us into a new vision of existence in the risen Christ.

2. Image of a renovated world

The celebration of the Eucharist creates a rich symbolic world to nourish the faith of the believing community. Archetypal symbols and images come into play to reveal to us a world transfigured by faith in Jesus Christ dead and raised to life in the Spirit. The participant in the liturgy enters into this world in which his own being is re-made, in which his heart and imagination are healed and refashioned.

Aidan Kavanagh describes the celebration of the Eucharist as offering the experience of a transfigured world, an experience which becomes the source of the Church's evangelizing proclamation:

It is as near to a description of, and a summons into, the world renovated according to God's pleasure as exists. It is the world seen in the light of Christ's gospel as a marriage feast, a table fellowship, in which God is the host, his Son the bridegroom, and we are the Spirited bride whose dowry is the life of the bridegroom himself. About the table all are gathered in free and equal association with the Source and Origin of all that is. And this is not just in spite of sin, but somehow, and mysteriously, because of that sin, that *felix culpa* which required so great a Redeemer[18].

The Eucharist was given to the Church in order to shape it according to the pattern of the *"new Man"*[19], Jesus the risen Lord. It is he who invites believers to God's table. He calls them to enter into the sway of his Passover mystery in order to share his gift of the Spirit. In him, God's redeemed world is taking shape; in him alone, the *"concrete universal"*[20], can humankind find its true identity. Drawn into the Trinitarian relationships by the power of the Spirit, the table fellows of Jesus the Lord enter into a process of personal and social transformation.

All the different aspects of the Eucharist converge upon this, that it fashions the participants into the image of the Lord:

Whoever eats my flesh and drinks my blood lives in me an I live in that person. As the living Father sent me and I draw life from the Father, so whoever eats me will also draw life from me[21].

This vision of a renovated world which comes to expression in the Eucharist is very rich. I wish to draw

---

[18] *Liturgy and Ecclesial Consciousness: A Dialectic of Change*, a talk given at the IX International Congress, Societas Liturgica, Vienna, 1983.

[19] Cf. Ep 4:23.

[20] Expression used by Hans Urs von Balthasar.

[21] Jn 6:56-57.

attention to several of its features which have special relevance to our experience today in a world passing through a vast cultural crisis, a crisis of ideals, in which models are in eclipse and values fragmented and without organic connection.

In particular, I wish to suggest how the Eucharist evangelizes our social existence, how it introduces us into God's wisdom, and how it creates hope in the new world of which it is an anticipation.

A. *God's community*

A Christian community is a unique gathering of people which owes its very existence to the free choice of God. The assembly gathered at the Eucharist is signed by the name of the Triune God from the beginning to the end of the celebration.

The community about God's table comes to know itself as the object of God's own desire. There are the worshippers whom the Father *"seeks"*, Jesus tells the Samaritan woman[22], using a very strong term[23]. He will speak at the Supper of his own desire te be at table with us. "I have ardently longed to eat this Passover with you before I suffer.[24]"

Jesus, in fact, saw his own death as the act whereby the Father would gather into one God's scattered

---

[22] Jn 4:23.

[23] See MATEOS, J. and J. BARRETO, *El Evangelio de Juan, Análisi Linguístico y Comentario Exegético*, Ediciones Cristiandad, Madrid, 1982, p. 239-240.

[24] Lk 22:15.

children[25]. The very being of the community, then, is inseparable from the memory of his life-giving death.

When Saint Paul declares that the celebration is a proclamation of the *death* of the Lord, he is not referring to a mere factual event. His references are best translated in terms of the *dying* of Jesus[26]. It is the inner attitude of Jesus which matters. The manner in which he died manifests his love, his fundamental attitude towards God his Father and towards people. In his *dying*, he assumed the consequences of his fidelity. He was *"handed over"*[27]. He gave his life into the hands of those who would destroy him. He consented to the will of his Father who allowed him to be handed over to the powers of evil, as Abraham had handed over his son to God's mysterious decree. This is the source of the fruitfulness of his dying. He allowed his Father to realize in his dying the mysterious transformation which is the deep law of all existence, namely the bringing of life *out of* death.

The principle whereby the assembly is constituted is not that of ordinary human affinities or common interest but it is God's free choice, a choice which is exercised in ways which may surprise us.

Chapter 14 of Saint Luke show us how disconcerting was the way Jesus called people into the Kingdom. On the occasion of a Sabbath meal at the house of a leading Pharisee, for example, Jesus perplexes his hearers when he tells them:

---

[25] Cf. Jn 17; 11:50.

[26] Jerome Murphy-O'Connor translates the expression in 2 Cor 4:10 not as *"the death of Jesus"*, but rather as *"the dying of Jesus"*, in *Becoming Human Together. The Pastoral Anthropology of Saint Paul*, Michael Glazier, Wilmington, Delaware, 1982, p. 45 ff.

[27] Cf. Mk 14:17-21.

When you give a lunch or a dinner, do not invite your friends or your brothers or your relations or rich neighbours, in case they invite you back and so repay you. No when you have a party, invite the poor, the crippled, the lame, the blind; then you will be blessed, for they have no means to repay you and so you will be repaid when the upright rise again[28].

There where the pharisees had excluded persons — the publican, for example, or the sinful woman or the man with dropsy — Jesus goes towards them, inviting them to enter into the new community of the Kingdom. He even goes so far as to propose them as models for the *"pious"* and the *"just"!*

God's surprising choice flows from his unique love *(agape)*, made present in our world by the life and especially the death of Jesus Christ. The Eucharistic assembly is called to make visible in its own manner of living the newness of this principle upon which its very existence is based, especially through its reaching out to those who are in some way distant and through the exercise of the new commandment which is the very heart of the Eucharist. In this it reveals the originality of the divine love. The Eucharist thereby brings into being a new form of social existence.

The community thus constituted lives, therefore, not by human sympathy and common interests but by the power of self-giving love. Its secret power is in *"sacrifice"*, namely the willingness to make available to the Father our gifts and energies, our life itself for the sake of the world, for his purposes and according to his ways of acting. In the Eucharist we understand

---

[28] Lk 14:12-14.

that doing the will of the Father is truly *"food"*[29] for us, source of incalculable joy and strength.

B. *The new wisdom*

In the second place, the Eucharist evangelizes by bringing us into contact with Christ in the power of his ressurection. As *"light of the nations"*[30], he teaches us a new wisdom. I wish to look at five aspects of this wisdom, namely: that it establishes us in the horizon of gratitude, it is a wisdom born of the Cross, which transforms desire, opens us to contemplation, and educates us to experience suffering redemptively.

Living in gratitude

The Eucharist establishes our lives within an horizon of gratitude, in which experience is seen as gift calling for a response in thankful praise. Even when faced with betrayal and death, Jesus is still able to give thanks. Thanksgiving is the constant horizon of his life. He is convinced that the Father is present in every aspect of his experience and he lives life as a constant dialogue with *Abba*. For him life is received as a gift; even the pain, which he does not want, is accepted if that be the Father's will.

The central act of the Eucharist is enshrined in the Eucharistic prayer or anaphora, which grew out of the basic unit of Jewish prayer. The essential module of Jewish prayer was the *"blessing"*, a prayer which

---

[29] Cf. Jn 4:31-34.
[30] Cf. Lk 2:32; Jn 8:12.

expressed the awareness that all of our experience is, first of all, gift, and so calls for a response of praise and thanksgiving[31]. This form of prayer which penetrated the whole life of the believer has been called the key to Jewish spirituality. For Louis Bouyer, it is *"the accomplished expression of the knowledge of God in the heart of the people."*[32] That Jesus prayed this way we know from the *hymn of jubilation* (referred to above) which we find in Matthew and Luke.

This attitude penetrated the religious awareness of Saint Paul, for example: *"Always be joyful"*, he writes, *"pray constantly; and for all things give thanks; this is the will of God for you in Christ Jesus."*[33] The Eucharistic prayer is the primary example and formative model of the believer's fundamental attitude towards existence.

This point is of crucial importance today. For we run the risk of falling into a new form of moralism when we insist, correctly, on the need for Christians to "become eucharist", that is to say, to "become bread broken" for their brothers and sisters. We will only perpetuate a moralistic mentality unless we make sure that becoming a gift for others is seen as a response born of a wonder-filled sense of the gratuitous character of one's own existence. Jesus did give himself, it is true; but *first* he received himself. He received his existence moment by moment as a gracious

---

[31] TALLEY, T.J., "The Eucharistic Prayer of the Ancient Church According to Recent Research: Results and Reflexions", *Studia Liturgica*, Vol. 11, 1976, p. 11-39.

[32] BOUYER, L., "Eucharist", *Theology and Spirituality of the Eucharistic Prayer*, University of Notre-Dame Press, Notre-Dame, 1968, Chapter 2.

[33] 1 Th 5:16-18.

and unmerited gift. He chose to return that gift by making available for the purposes of God his Father his energy, his intelligence, his power to love, rather than in the pursuit of any interest exclusively focused on his own self.

Here we see the profound truth in Irenaeus' observation, that God gave the disciples the Eucharist *"lest they be ungrateful and sterile."*[34] For thanksgiving or gratitude is the source of fruitfulness. Giving thanks is not just a formula of words. It is a recognition in faith of the presence of God at the heart of all experience; it is the ability to see all experience as a gift from a good God, who allows us to experience all that we experience for life and not for diminishment.

A "eucharistic people", accustomed to praise and thank God in all circumstances, is able to witness to a source of joy which is not to be found in the consumer society which surrounds us. This brings us to another trait of much importance for evangelization.

The wisdom of the cross

A people evangelized by the Sacrament is a people which lives by wisdom, not its own wisdom, but the *"wisdom that is from above"*[35], the wisdom that is a gift from the Lord, the *"wisdom of the cross."*[36]

In the face of the religious cultures of his day, Paul discovered that the message he carried aroused disappointment. A crucified Saviour seemed to the Greeks

---

[34] "Adversus Haereses", IV, 17,5, *Sources chrétiennes,* no. 100, Cerf, Paris, 1965, p. 591-592.

[35] Jm 3:15.

[36] 1 Cor 1:17 — 2; 16.

no answer to their search for wisdom; it struck them rather as rank folly. Nor did it satisfy Jewish expectations either. In the light of their dream of a powerful leader who would usher in God's kingdom with power, the message seemed intolerable weakness. The same message hardly fares any better today.

Since the Enlightenment, people have tended to place their hopes in knowledge or science, penetrating the secrets of the universe, and in technology, giving us control over our world. We might well add a third expectation, common in our culture, the search for happiness through the expansion of experience — whether it be sexual experience, psychic experience through drugs, or mystical experience through meditation or occult practices and the like. For human hopes focused on the conquests of knowledge, power and experience, the Gospel message seems no less forbidding than formerly.

Many *"seekers"* in our time, marked as it is by the *"return of religion"* and the rumoured advent of a *"New Age"*, are looking for some kind of lost paradise, which they hope, often enough, to find in secret knowledge, psychic or spiritual power or enlarged experience. For them too the message of the Cross comes across as folly, weakness or unacceptable harshness. The Eucharist, by contrast, invites us to ponder the Cross, to *"eat the flesh of the Son of Man and drink his blood"*[37], namely to nourish ourselves with the strangely bitter bread and drink of God till it transforms our outlook and re-creates our minds. It evokes the great images of the seed which dies in order to bring forth new life, of the lamb of God, of the cross

---

[37] Jn 6:53.

that is the sign of victory — the manifold images and strange ironies of the Gospel which ease our minds into the rare and singular truth. It teaches us the true wisdom, which is the knowledge of God and his ways in the world; it enables us to experience the true power which is, in faith, to be able *"to do all things in him who strengthens me."*[38]

Only when we pay heed to such wisdom will we be able to use the riches of science and technology for the true good of humankind.

Transformation of desire

Human experience in our time has undergone an extraordinary enlargement. Expectations for life and happiness which pre-modern people would never have dreamed of entertaining, have become, through the vast spread of the media, those of the masses. The modern person tends, in consequence, to be dissatisfied and restless. Our inability to accept our situation and to be at peace with ourselves and our world, of course, is nothing new; but today it is surely exacerbated. Something of this appears clearly in the debate Jesus had with the Jews after the multiplication of the loaves. The eucharistic discourse shows the people restlessly yearning for easy bread and Jesus seeking to draw them to something higher. They are dissatisfied, however, and manifest an attitude which is the very opposite of the eucharistic attitude, namely one of *"murmuring"*. Fundamentally, this expression denotes an inability to accept the conditions in which God places us.

---

[38] Ph 4:13.

This attitude of *"murmuring"* finds its classic expression in the Exodus. The people were dissatisfied with their lot. God sent them food and they thought only to indulge their craving. Failing to perceive that *"man does not live on bread alone, but on every word that comes from the mouth of God"*[39], they died in large numbers. The place came to be known as *"the graves of craving"*[40] and the incident took on emblematic value in the Biblical tradition.

Jesus seeks to lead the people beyond their own fixed ideas of happiness, beyond their rigid expectations of what God should provide for them. He admonishes them to work for a bread which will last and will save them from death. He himself is this bread; the new manna will take the form of his own body and blood, as true food and drink, and is accessible only to faith. What we see here is the invitation to grow, to put one's own ideas into question, to allow oneself to be led by God. A community which celebrates the Eucharist frequently should be a community which is acquiring a taste for God's bread.

The Eucharist is, then, a school for desire. It represents not a denial of desire, but the opening of it to its fulfillment. The pedagogy of desire, though, must necessarily pass through a painful phase of negation. For our diet of unwholesome nourishment, such as an attachment to the need for power or for the pursuit of prestige or money as sources of worth and value, destroys our taste for true bread. We need to acquire a taste for what is wholesome, which entails our undergoing the experience of God's "otherness", his

---

[39] Dt 8:3.
[40] Nb 11:34.

holiness. Meeting the real God, and not an idol, will mean the frustration of the desires we project upon him. Yet if the withdrawal symptoms provoked by our letting go of our addictions can be very painful, they are a sign that the door of transformation is opening for us.

The Eucharist reveals little by little the only experience that can truly fill the heart.

Contemplation

Much Christian mysticism has been associated with the Eucharist. John on Patmos has his vision of the victorious Jesus on *"the first day of the week"*[41], the Lord's day, which exegetes say evokes the Eucharist. The greatest mystery takes place not in solitude, far from human company, but in the midst of the gathered community. Jesus revealed his paschal mystery and unfolded the deepest revelation of his relationship with the Father at his Last Supper with his disciples. The sacred, for the Christian, in an economy of incarnation, finds its place at the very heart of one of the most basic human experiences, that of having a meal, of eating together. We see this already foreshadowed in the mysterious story of Moses and the seventy elders of Israel who feast with God on the mountain. Their mystical experience is conveyed by a strange image. For *"they saw"*, says the author, *"the God of Israel beneath whose feet there was what looked like a sapphire pavement pure as the heavens themselves."*

---

[41] Rev 1:10.

Astonished, he repeats, *"they actually gazed on God and then ate and drank."*[42]

This scene reminds us of Philip's eager plea to Jesus at the Last Supper, *"Lord, show us the Father and then we shall be satisfied."*[43] In his reply, Jesus identifies the place of contact with the Father, *"Anyone who has seen me has seen the Father."*[44] The meeting with the Father takes place at the table where we gather with Jesus. In the breaking of bread our eyes will be opened and we will recognize Jesus.

This contemplative dimension of the liturgy calls for moments of silence and the avoidance of excessive verbalization, which is all too common today. Particularly important moments for such silence are the proclamation of the readings and of the Eucharistic prayer. The properly objective character of the liturgy must be respected if its full power is to be unleashed. For the mystical dimension of the celebration may be closed off by an excessive personalization in the manner of celebration, whereby the personality of the celebrant or the subjective concerns of the assembly are allowed to dominate.

Eucharistic adoration can be seen as a prolonging of this contemplative moment or dimension of the celebration. It is a way of *dwelling* in the mystery, whereby we "replay" it in order to taste the goodness of the Lord and to place ourselves at his disposal so that he may be formed in us. Today, with the recovery of interest in contemplative prayer and the revival of the practice of Eucharistic adoration, the possibility of

---

[42] Ex 24:10-11.

[43] Jn 14:8.

[44] Jn 14:9.

a deeper interiorization of the Eucharist is becoming available to many people.

Redemptive suffering

The wisdom of a eucharistic people is particularly evident where it is question of coping with suffering. Wonderful advances in science and technology have enabled us to diminish the amount of pain in people's lives, but they have also made it increasingly difficult to know how to deal with pain. Easy recourse to barbiturates has become a common way of fleeing the uncomfortable experience of anxiety, of doubt, guilt and restless dissatisfaction. Addictions of many kinds afflict our society.

The Eucharist evangelizes our experience of suffering, schooling us in seeing the redemptive dimension of pain. This statement is not to be understood, of course, whithin the "doloristic" perspectives of some unwholesome spiritualities of the past, but as the joyous affirmation not only that pain is not the last word in life, but that it can be transformed into life-giving power. For, thanks to Baptism, the resurrection is already at work in our mortal being.

The sending of the Eucharist bread to the sick and the house-bound elderly, for example, is not simply a gesture of charity and inclusion on the part of the Eucharistic assembly. It is also an affirmation of their redemptive role in the sacrifice that they celebrate in the Eucharist. It teaches them to fulfill in their bodies that which is lacking in them of their participation in the sufferings of Christ[45]. This simple act reveals the

---

[45] Col 1:24.

paschal faith of the gathered community, which sees in every human life the possibility of participating in the paschal mystery[46]. As Sacrament of the paschal mystery, therefore, the Eucharist brings us into the presence of the world of suffering — of the lonely and the handicapped and incapacitated of every kind — whether their sufferings be spiritual, mental or physical.

Similarly, before the inexplicable tragedies, the suffering of the innocent, the appalling injustices without redress, the Eucharist brings us constantly face to face with the atrocious suffering of the innocent Just One, massacred with judicial approval because he had challenged the power of the mighty. The Eucharist teaches us to deal with our brokenness and the unfinished character of human life. The victorious Jesus offers us his own broken body to make us whole, he displays his own wounds to heal us[47]. In the face of our broken promises and the fragility of our commitments he offers us, in the heart of his own apparent abandonment by his Father, *"a new and eternal covenant"* sealed with the faithful God who brings life out of death.

To sum up, then, the Eucharist evangelizes our social existence, and it brings us the light of a new wisdom, establishing the horizon of gratitude, teaching us the wisdom of the Cross, transforming desire,

---

[46] See *Gaudium et spes*, no. 22.

[47] With the advent of the new freedom in Eastern Europe and elsewhere, we hear once again of the power of the Eucharist celebrated with jealously harboured fragments of bread and a few drops of wine in the prisons, the concentration camps for ideological re-education.

leading us into contemplation and revealing to us the redemptive value of suffering.

In the third place, the Eucharist evangelizes by giving hope.

3. Hope for the world

Jesus lived his Passover in an attitude of intense waiting for the Kingdom[48]. His Eucharist is marked by the same ardent expectation. Every celebration is situated between the past of Jesus' Passover, the today of the community's life and the tomorrow of the Lord's coming. This is expressed in the ancient prayer *Marana tha!*[49]

A eucharistic people is one which participates with unwavering hope in the building up of a society of justice and brothersisterhood, *"a civilization of love"*, to use the expression of Pope Paul VI. The Christian is called to play his part in preparing the table for the universal banquet[50]. Especially in times of great stress and change like ours, the Christian is willing to give himself to the task despite the failures and partial achievements, because he is convinced that no fragment of human effort is lost, that what he offers each Sunday in the Eucharist is being gathered by God as part of his Kingdom[51].

A Eucharistic people is also a people whose hope enables them to create utopian signs. Amongst the

---

[48] Cf. Lk 22:16-18.

[49] 1 Cor 16:22; Rev 22:20.

[50] As Paul VI said in his celebrated discourse to the United Nations.

[51] See *Gaudium et spes*, no. 39.

sinking examples of recent times I think of Assisi, where Pope John Paul II gathered leaders of all religions to pray for peace.

Another example is provided by the community of Sant'Egidio in Rome. Each year at Christmas the community invites the poor people whom it serves to a banquet in the church of Santa Maria in Trastevere. Tables are set up, gypsies and the lonely elderly, vagabonds and those who have no place in society are seated at them, to be served as honoured guests. This seems to me an eloquent symbol, analogous in its way to the prophetic act of the multiplication of the loaves performed by Jesus. It is true because it arises out of concrete daily service of the poor. Its symbolic content, it seems to me, consists in this. For notwithstanding all that we do, sickness, human failure and inadequacy, the multiple and innumerable tragedies of human life continue. The poor will always be with us. Yet something new is present in our midst and it is essential for the Church to offer signs that bring it to expression. Such signs speak of the coming Kingdom, they enable us to glimpse what is beyond but which is coming to birth in our midst already. They foreshadow the banquet of the Kindgom and are profoundly eucharistic: for they are born of the Eucharist and reveal its inner logic, its transforming drive.

A Eucharistic Congress can also be the occasion of such signs[52]. People gather from many parts of the world about the Eucharist to celebrate and reflect upon this mystery through which God is transforming our existence. The *agape* during the Congress or

---

[52] Cf. PRATZNER, Ferdinand, in *The International Eucharistic Congresses. For a New Evangelization*, Vatican City, 1991, [Part: Origin and Development, p. 7-59).

the gift of blood (as in the Congress of Seoul), however modest as signs, do make visible something of the inner dynamism of the Sacrament. We may be reminded by such signs of Isaiah's vision of the mountain where people *"will hammer their swords into ploughshares and their spears into sickles"*[53], for war will be no more. This is the place of God's banquet.

The efforts of Christians (and others) to contribute to the construction of a more just and fraternal world is not the futile labour of a Sisyphus, but the building of an eternal kingdom, a new heaven and a new earth which every Eucharistic celebration proclaims and of which it is sign and foretaste.

---

[53] Is 2:4.

THE EUCHARIST: SUMMONS AND STIMULUS, CALL AND CHALLENGE TO EVANGELIZATION: THE EUCHARIST AS A MISSIONARY EVENT

Cardinal Jaime L. Sin
Archbishop of Manille

Introduction

To speak of the Eucharist as a permanent impetus, a summons and stimulus to evangelization, a call and challenge to mission, is to see "the Eucharist as a missionary event". It is a challenging theme to enter into, and yet it is a deeply true one.

I

That great event of the Christian history of our time, the Second Vatican Council, has taught us that the Church is "like a Sacrament, a sign, an instrument of intimate oneness with God, and of the Unity of the whole human race."[1] Thus, the Church is ultimately about bringing oneness into humanity; perhaps bet-

---

[1] *Lumen gentium*, no. 1.

ter, bringing humanity into oneness. We speak here of a unity rooted in oneness with God, whose source is the one life of the Father, the Son and the Spirit. The Church is ultimately, about shaping human history into a journey towards human community in "communion" (koinonia); a communion which is one in the power, the life and the love of the spirit of God.

The condition of the modern world (the Council goes on to say) lends even greater urgency to this duty of the Church: for while men of the present day are drawn ever more closely together by social, technical and cultural bonds, it still remains for them to achieve full unity in Chirst[2].

We are reminded of that grand image of Saint Augustine of "Adam broken up and gathered together", from one of his sermons on the psalms.

"For with righteousness shall He judge the world." Not a part of it only, for it was not merely a part that He redeemed [...] He paid the price for the whole world. You have heard what the Gospel has to say, that when He comes "He shall gather together the elect from the four winds" (Mk 13:27), that is to say, from the whole world.

Now Adam's name... means in Greek, the whole world. Fore there are four letters, A, D, A, M, and with the Greeks the four quarters of the world have these initial letters. They are East, "Anatolia"; the West, "Dusis"; the North, "Arctus"; and the South, "Mesembria". A, D, A, M: these letters spell ADAM. ADAM is thus scattered throughout the globe. Set in

---

[2] *Ibid.*

one place, he fell, as it were broken small, he has filled the whole world. But the Divine Mercy gathered up the fragments from every side, forged them in the fire of love, and welded into one what had been broken.

That was a work which this artist knew how to do; let no one therefore give way to despair. An immense task it was indeed, but think who the artist was. He who remade it was himself the maker; he who refashioned it was himself the fashioner. "He shall judge the world in righteousness and the nations in His Truth"[3].

Let us begin with that vision, of "Adam broken up and gathered together". For this is the great ecclesial task, the missionary agenda which we must place before us. The Eucharist, we know, not only impels us to it; it is also the great symbol of its realization, "the shape of things to be, and (as we have said) summons and stimulus, but also the power, the energy by which it will come to fulfillment.

II

If, in the development of the Church's life over the centuries, Word and Sacrament sometimes became divided realities, with some Churches (especially after the Reformation) concentrating on the proclamation of the Word, and others centered around the Sacraments, above all the Eucharist, the Council insisted that these two must never be separated. Once again the Constitution on the Church speaks clearly here:

---

[3] *On Psalm 95*, Migne: PL 37, 1236.

For the Church is driven by the Holy Spirit to do her part for the full realization of the plan of God, who has constituted Christ as the source of salvation for the whole world. By her proclamation of the Gospel, she draws her hearers to receive and profess the faith, she prepares them for Baptism, snatches them from the slavery of error, and she incorporates them into Christ, so that in love for Him they grow to full maturity.

The effect of her work is that whatever good is found sown in the minds and hearts of men, or in the rites and customs of peoples, they are not only preserved from destruction, but are purified, raised up and perfected for the glory of God, the confusion of the devil, and the happiness of men.

Each disciple of Christ has the obligation of spreading the faith to the best of his ability. But if any believer can baptize, it is for the priests *to complete the building up of the Body in the Eucharistic sacrifice*, fulfilling the words of the prophet. "From the rising of the sun, even to its going down, my name is great among the Gentiles. And in every place there is a sacrifice, and there is offered to my name a clean offering." (Ml 1:11)[4]

In the task of announcing the Gospel, the Word proclaimed and the Supper celebrated are constitutive, "and thus, the Eucharist was a basic dimension of the missionary task of the Church from the very beginning". The Word is proclaimed, so that the body might be built up. Thus theologians today, in a happy turn of phrase, speak of the Eucharist as "the maxi-

---

[4] *Lumen gentium*, nos. 11, 17.

mum densification of the Word."[5] The Decree *Ad gentes* puts the same thought in a somewhat different way.

> Through the preaching of the Word, and the celebration of the Sacraments, whose center and culmination is the most Holy Eucharist, Christ is made present, Christ the author of salvation[6].

Again, Word and Sacrament are constitutive dimensions of evangelization. The Eucharist is at the core of the proclamation of the Good News, because when the Eucharist is celebrated, *that* which is proclaimed, better still, He who is proclaimed and whose great deed announced to all, is made present: preaching yields presence. From the Lord's presence, the redemption that he accomplishes, is poured out upon the world. It is the Eucharist, finally, which re-creates the broken Adam, and fashions him into one body of Christ in the Church and in the world.

III

All of God's gifts are tasks; thus does God honor us and our freedom. The Eucharist is gift, in the words we treasure in our liturgy.

> *In quo Christus sumitur*
> *Mens impletur gratia,*
> *Et futurae gloriae nobis pignus datur.*

---

[5] *Rahner, Bruno Forte.*

[6] *Ad gentes*, no. 9.

The Eucharist is that sacred banquet (*sacrum convivium*) in which the "subversive memory" of the passion and cross is renewed for us and in us; the crucified and risen Christ is present in our lives and in the world, and we are given the pledge and earnest of what we yet await in the glory of the Kingdom. *Christus in nobis, spes gloriae.*

Much of what I would to say here is found in the *First Letter to the Corinthians:*

> In the first place, I hear that when you all come together as a community, there are separate factions among you, and I half believe it [...] The point is, when you hold these meetings, it is not the Lord's Supper that you are eating, since when the time comes to eat, everyone is in such a hurry to start his own supper that one person goes hungry, while another is getting drunk. Surely, you have enough homes for eating and drinking in? Surely you have enough respect for the community of God not to make poor people embarrassed?

> [...] Until the Lord comes, therefore, every time you eat this bread and drink this cup, you are proclaiming His death, and so anyone who eats the bread and drinks the cup of the Lord unworthily will be behaving unworthily towards the body and blood of the Lord.

> Everyone is to recollect himself before eating this bread and drinking this cup, because a person who eats and drinks without recognizing the body, eats and drinks his own condemnation.[7]

---

[7] 1 Cor 11:18-29.

It is clear, that Paul's words here are spoken into a context of faction and division, a context (it has been called) of "contempt for community". He confronts estrangement, seemingly accepted, between rich and poor, as "a fact of life". Paul says, the Eucharist is meant to be a meal of *koinonia,* whose most authentic expression it is. In its celebration, to sin against community is to sin against the body and blood of Christ[8].

Whenever we eat this bread and drink this cup, we proclaim the death of the Lord; a sacrifice for our reconciliation and brotherhood. Thus the Eucharist is "the place of all places for recalling Jesus' own gift of self for the ending of all our estrangements and divisions. The Eucharist proclaims the end of all barriers of sinful separation of any kind. It gives us the power by which all wounds in the body of the new Adam may be healed.

Rightly then does the Eucharist challenge us to ask: What are the "sins against community" which communion in the Lord's body commands us to do combat against, in ourselves and in society? Where are the gaping wounds which the Eucharist lays bare before our eyes?

Saint Paul's words to the Corinthians single out "making the poor embarrassed" — the example stands surely for other things too. But do we not too complacently, indifferently, accept the division between the wealthy of this world and the poor — not between individuals only, but between social groupings, between peoples and nations? When we come together for Eucharist, does not this intolerable sin against

---

[8] Cf. MALONEY, F.J., SDB, *A Body for a Broken People,* Sydney, Collins-Dove, 1990, p. 110-117.

community bring us any anguish at all, any pain? Does the Eucharist we receive hold up before us the imperative (yes, on each of us!) to do all that is possible, to break the bonds of poverty, to find ways of changing the relationships, the systems entrenched, which perpetuate this fundamental division, across the worldwide Church, and across the world? The refusal to live out, to realize, communion, — my brothers and sisters here present, I know you have heard all this before, and perhaps are weary of hearing it. But as we gather here, representing the *oecumene* of the Christian world, how can we not cry out again, in the name of the Gospel and Eucharist, no matter how much it may offend? In the affluence we see around us, even now at a time of worldwide recession, must not this message be shouted again, from the housetops?

There are many ways by which "one person goes hungry, while another has already had too much to drink." There are the division wrought by racism in open, or subtly hidden, ways. Apartheid may be officially and legally dead on paper, but it is really alive and well. It goes by other names like "ethnic cleansing", in wars like the one which ravages a land not far from here. There are ages-old oppressions of women in every so-called "civilization" in history; even today the struggle for *their* dignity, in so many places, has only just begun. There are innumerable stratagems of social, economic and political domination and exploitation, on every level of human relations that we can only speak in general terms. The Eucharist proclaims the unacceptability of all of these before the cross of Jesus, before His death which we announce.

The Eucharist denounces this multi-headed "contempt for koinonia", by its very nature, and announces that it itself is the way for healing our woundedness. When we gather for Eucharist, we must learn to look for those who are "on the under-side of history", and teach ourselves to realize that Christ in His sacrifice makes their lowliness and bro-kenness and victimhood His own, that all of it He bears in His own body.

The young girls sold into sexual slavery in so many cities in Asia; boys made prostitutes so they can earn a living for their families — Oh, we have dozens of them, aged seven upwards catering to men from the First World! I think of Steve Biko stripped naked and brought dying in a police van over bumpy roads to his Golgotha. Only yesterday I know children were handed over for slave labor in lands neighboring mine. And today — today, not in Dicken's century — mineworkers in their late teens cough away in airless tunnels.

Enough, — but you see, Christ makes all their woundedness and their victimhood His own, in the Eucharist. When we say *Amen* to the *Body of Christ* in communion, we place ourselves in solidarity with that Christ "who bears all these in Himself". And thus we must with Him place ourselves in solidarity with all the suffering and brokenness in the world. My brothers and sisters, this is not pious rhetoric: It is the mystery of our Christ in the Eucharist!

The body of Christ, broken for the world, is not only the assurance of our forgiveness. It is also the decla-ration of God's love for the whole world. To partake of that body is to share in "the suffering of God". It is

123

an expression of solidarity with God and with all the children of God[9].

In saying Amen to the Body of Christ, we say Amen to our responsibility for all those whose lives Christ has taken up into His own body. It has been powerfully argued that this meaning is also intrinsic to our Eucharistic Communion.

> We take brokennes into ourselves, and it becomes part of us. And as Jesus had offered Himself as covenant so that all could have access to Him, somehow our lives have to be lived so that, as a result, as many people as possible can be brought into a deeper sharing in the earth's resources, that they may become more fully the image of God that they are meant to be. Our *Amen* has to be a commitment to bind up wounds, to heal the broken, to enable all to have access to life, — or else they become empty words.

> We must become the sacramental reality if it is to be real in our lives. In the case of the Eucharist, we are to become the covenant, the body broken that others may be healed, the blood poured out that others may have access to life[10].

Thus the Eucharist tells us that to evangelize is "to take upon ourselves the role of the servant."[11] The other great image of the Last Supper comes to mind here. It is that of Jesus washing the feet of the apostles.

---

[9] *Emilio Castro.*

[10] CROSBY, Michael, OFM Cap., *Thy Will Be Done*, New York, Orbis, 1977, p. 130-131.

[11] Cf. Isaiah.

Thus Jesus says to them: To announce the Gospel is to give witness to a love that gives itself even unto death. To receive the Eucharist is to share in the vocation of the servant. Thus the Church is called to "mission as service" for the liberation of our brothers; called to love "to the uttermost limits of loving."[12]

Thus the spirit awakens charisms for ministry in the Church: Those for the ordained ministry, those whose lives find their meaning in representing the shepherding Christ who gives His life for His sheep. But today, most of all, the spirit awakens incredible generosity among lay people, among the young, — people whose generosity shames us by its totality, whose self-giving takes our breath away. If there is so much suffering and poverty in our world, still Eucharist and Spirit renew the Church with disciples who are not afraid to follow the Lord wherever He leads them.

IV

There is yet another wound which lacerates the body of Christ, the on-going division among our Churches. We are reminded that 30 years ago this week, on 3 June 1963, the beloved Pope John XXIII died. He died, you will remember, offering his life with the last anguished longing of the Lord, *Ut unum sint*, spoken over and over again in his last hours. I remember reading, in the words taken down by those around his bedside, on 30 May, how often that prayer was uttered.

---

[12] Jn 13:1.

Perhaps in the intervening 30 years we have lost Pope John's passion for healing that open wound in the Church. But now, as we gather here, must we not experience again the pain of broken community? The entire patristic and medieval tradition taught us that the unity of the body of Christ is the *res* — the full fruitfulness — of the Eucharist. Here, as we recall Angelo Roncalli's death, must we not rekindle our passion, *Ut unum sint?* After so many centuries, we cannot yet share a common table for those who believe in Christ, even in the midst of unbelief and practical atheism surrounding us. At least let us pray, with the anguish of good Pope John, that this division may be healed.

In this connection, may I add one point. Those of us who are here from beyond European boundaries want to remind our brethren here that it was people from your shores who brought from the North, brought to us, the divisions of Christendom, the broken relationship which sunder Christ's body. They were not of our making, you brought them to us; they are the heritage of our past. Unless you undo them *here* among yourselves, how shall they be healed among us? Who is responsible finally, for keeping them alive? Here at this Congress, let Jesus' longing, let Pope John's anguished hope, pass through our hearts. The Eucharist challenges us to this, at this hour of grace.

V

But the Eucharist asks even more from us, more of "the unfinished business of the Kingdom". *Redemptoris missio* has reminded us that evangelization, even "first evangelization", remains a crucial imperative for our time. Recent figures tell us that 23 percent of the people in the *world today* have no knowledge of Christ and His Gospel: 1.2 billion people! (The figure was, it seems, 330 million in 1491, when Christopher Columbus sailed across the Atlantic. Five hundred years later, the figure is at leat four times larger!) And each year an additional 145 million come into the world, of whom some 50 million will almost surely never come to contact with Christ and his Church. In Asia, we Christians form about three percent of the total population. If our absolute numbers are, in fact, growing, still "unbelievers" grow in numbers also, as do those who belong to other religious traditions. "The race goes against us."

How are we, as Church, to meet this situation? Since its First Plenary Assembly in Taipeh in 1974, the Federation of Asian Bishops' Conference (FABC) has been struggling with that question: Evangelization in Asia in our time. The bishops then spoke of *"Building up the Local Church"* as the fundamental demand of evangelization, in our part of the world. Most of us were emerging from the status of "colonial missions" and taking first unsteady steps, on our own, to become *ecclesiae novellae*, "young Churches". Churches coming into consciousness as Church, as "becoming Church". Churches on the way to becoming ecclesial subjects of their own self-realization, in the great communion of Churches which is the Church universal, the *Catholica*. The Second Vatican Council has taught us so much about the Church!

But the deepest source of our "becoming Church" was, and is, the Eucharist. We have that great principle of the tradition, already a common principle of the Fathers of the Church: *Ecclesia facit Eucharistiam, Eucharistia facit Ecclesiam.* It is the community, gathering together which — in the Spirit — actualizes the Eucharist. And it is the Eucharist, the crucified and risen Lord taking the community and its sacrifices to Himself, which makes the Church. Thus the Eucharist makes the local Church. The great preacher, Bossuet, had said, "Jesus bears us in Himself. We are, if I may dare say so, so more truly His body than His own body."[13] Christ bears us in Himself in the Eucharist. *Eucharistia facit Ecclesiam.*

The Asian bishops have spoken again and again of the three dialogues through the proclamation of Christ and His Gospel is to be carried out. Nowhere do they say that dialogue replaces proclamation: proclamation of Jesus Christ is what the Church's mission is about. But in Asia, proclamation must follow the path of dialogue. Pope Paul VI in his encyclical *Ecclesiam suam* had shown us the way; it was, from him that the FABC drew the theme, "The Dialogue of Life".

This means, an immersion in the total reality of our peoples' lives, their religious traditions, their cultures, their real situations of poverty and struggle for humanity, justice and peace... Is this not the way the Son of God came to us in the Incarnation? His immersion in our human condition was complete, sin alone excepted. And is not the Eucharist a prolongation of this same logic of Incarnation? Is not the way of the Eucharist also a Dialogue of Life, casting of his lot with ours, a total sharing of what He is for us, so that

---

[13] Cf. De LUBAC, H., *Catholicism,* London, Sheed and Ward, 1947, p. 44.

"He may bear us in Himself." And make all of us His one body?

One of the dialogue areas in evangelization has come to be known as "inculturation". Does not the Eucharist embody the principle of inculturation in its reality? Food and drink, drawn from our earth and the work of our own hands, the breaking of bread we have made, the sharing of the one cup of wine, is not our banquet itself Christ making our human meals His own, He, assuming all our human life and human labor, human communion, into Himself and what He does for us? Is not our human diversity thus invited to enter into His Eucharist and our own?

The diversity of human cultures, of human languages and histories and traditions, can, of course, be hindrances to communion among peoples, blockages to the unity we seek across the face of the earth. The story of the Tower of Babel is a dramatic symbol of that. But diversities are, first of all, the expression of human richness, of the infinite variety of human resources and human gifts. Diversity need not stand in the way of communion. It can, in fact, be an invitation to communion, enrichment of community, Joseph's lovely coat of many colors. Thus *Lumen gentium* (no. 13) puts the fostering of diversity within the *Catholic Unitas* which is the Church, one of the

---

[14] Note: In this section we have followed closely the exegesis of texts given by the Biblical scholar Joachim Jeremias, in his well-known study, *Jesus' Promise to the Nations*, London, SCM Press, 1958. Also Donald Senior, CP, Carroll Stuhlmueller, CP, *The Biblical Foundations for Mission*, Maryknoll, New York, Orbis, 1983.

crucial tasks of the ministry of Peter in the Communion of Churches.

As we dwell a little more fully on inculturation as a perspective on evangelization, we will grasp more deeply the meaning of "the Eucharist, as a missionary event."

Sometimes people may speak of inculturation as if it were merely a strategy or tactic for evangelism. No it is not that, unless one were to consider the Incarnation of God's Son merely a tactic also. Inculturation of Gospel and Christian life is continuing the way the Son took, in becoming Emmanuel, God-with-us. Inculturation is a "following through" of the way of Jesus. We must insert its notion in the total panorama of mission.

Today I will touch on one theme only, that of the *Eschathological Pilgrimage of the Nations to the Holy Mountain of God.* We may begin by recalling one scripture text which Jesus read in the Bible, and would refer to in his teaching:

> And it shall come to pass in the latter days, that the mountain of the Lord's house shall be established on the top of the mountains, and it shall be exalted above the hills. And all nations shall flow into it, and many peoples shall come and say, come ye, let us go up to the mountain of the Lord, to the house of the God of Jacob, and he will teach us his ways, and he will walk in his paths. (Is 2:2 ff., par. in Mi 4:1 ff.)[15]

This text, Biblical scholars (like Joachim Jeremias) tells us, describes to us the *Epiphany of God*, made

---

[15] JEREMIAS, J., *Jesus' Promise to the Nations*, London, SCM, 1959, p. 56.

visible to all the nations: God's glory is being revealed to all the world[16]. This epiphany of God is *accompanied by His word:* "God, even God the Lord hath spoken, and called the earth from the rising of the sun, unto its setting."[17] And God says to the Gentiles:

> Assemble yourselves and come, draw near together, ye that are escaped of the nations [...] look unto me and be ye saved, all the ends of the earth: for I am God, and there is no one else[18].

> Declare His glory among the nations (so the psalmist cries out), His marvelous works among all the peoples [...] says among the nations, *the Lord reigns!*[19]

And lastly, God sends His servant, who is to restore Israel, and whom God makes known as the light of all peoples[20]. (Let us recall that the opening lines of *Lumen gentium* come from these texts: *Lumen gentium cum sit Christus...*)

> I have formed you and appointed you, to be a light to all peoples, a beacon for the nations, to open eyes that are blind, to bring captives out of prison, out of the dungeons where they lie in darkness.

This is the first moment of mission, a "Centrifugal Moment", if you wish, God's messengers go forth, from the shining-forth of God's glory on the mountain, bearing the call of God on all the roads of the

---

[16] Is 40:5.
[17] Ps 50:1.
[18] Is 45:20-22.
[19] Ps 96:3-10.
[20] Is 42:6; 49:6.

world, to the very ends of the earth, to proclaim God's word inviting all peoples to the Holy Mountain.

Then there is a *second moment*, a "centripetal" one: the response of the nations; peoples journeying to God. "Come ye, let us go to the mountain of the Lord."[21] "A road is constructed, a highway straight through the near east, from Egypt and Assyria to Jerusalem."[22] The great pilgrimage of all humanity is on its way.

We all know that marvelous text we read in the liturgy of the Feast of the Epiphany, the passage from Isaiah which rings like a triumphant hymn of joy:

> The nations come to your light and the kings to your dawning brightness. Lift up your eyes and look around: All are assembling, all are coming toward you: your sons from far away, and your daughters, tenderly carried [...] The riches of the sea will flow to you, the wealth of the nations come to you. Camels in throngs will cover you, and dromedaries of Midian and Ephah. Everyone in Sheba will come, bringing gold and incense, and singing the praise of the Lord[23].

What an exultant vision! (And does it not speak to us here, at this Eucharistic Congress which is a gathering of nations?)

All the peoples come, led by their kings. This splendid caravan, almost like a circus parade in its variety: horses, mules, camels, dromedaries, litters, chariots... What have you. Joy, for the word has gone

---

[21] Is 2:3.

[22] Is 19:23.

[23] Is 60:1-6.

forth, and the word has been heard! Joy, for now they come, bringing their gifts to God. Every sort of gift, in overflowing: the peoples backs are bent, Isaiah tells us, with the weight of their precious cargo![24] The riches from the sea: shining pearls and treasures of the deep; gold and silver, incense and rarest oils; animals ready to be sacrificed; costly, fragrant woods to build the temple, and even the most valuable of all, children, carried in arms. Upwards they stream, up to the mountain of God, Jerusalem the great city[25]. Endlessly they come: the gates must be kept open day and night, "that men may bring unto thee the wealth of the nations."[26]

And what is this wealth of the nations? May we not say, the gifts of peoples' cultures? What people create with their minds and hands, from earth and sea and sky: "Fruits of the earth and the labor of men's hands." Songs and stories, arts and thought and troves of wisdom: gifts of the cultures of humanity. Human cultures gather the best and deepest which the humanity of nations produce. If cultures are peoples' ways of being human, if they contain the unsearchable riches of humanity throughout the world, and over the long reaches of time, then these are the gifts of the kings, gifts that bend the shoulders of their bearers, the backs of beasts of burden. There are the gifts of the nations, their very own, because they are the gifts of their thanksgiving and the tributes of their wondering, rejoicing love!

---

[24] Is 18:7; Ps 68:30-32.
[25] Is 60:11.
[26] Is 66:20.

And where do these endless streams of pilgrims go? To worhisp the Lord.

> Even them [the Gentiles] will I bring to my Holy Mountain, and make them joyful in my house of prayer; their burnt offerings and sacrifices shall be accepted upon my altar: for my house shall be called a house of prayer for all the peoples of the earth[27].

But this is not all: the worship shall culminate in the great Messianic Banquet, there upon the Holy Mountain.

> And in this mountain shall the Lord of Hosts make unto all peoples a feast of fat things, a feast of wines on the lees [...] and he will destroy on this mountain the face of the covering that is cast over all peoples, and the veil that is spread over all nations. He will destroy death forever[28].

There, upon the Holy Mountain, all peoples shall hold festival before the Lord. They shall be, all of them, God's chosen people. They shall behold the face of their God, and they shall be His people. God will cleanse their lips[29], and they will proclaim God upon cleansed lips. "For thou are great, thou doest wondrous things, thou who art God alone![30] And God responds: as the peoples worship Him, He pronounces them the "amazing blessing, transcending all national boundaries": 'Blessed be Egypt, my people;

---

[27] Is 56:7; cf. Mk 11:17.

[28] Is 25:6-8.

[29] Zp 3:9.

[30] Ps 86:10.

Assyria, the work of my hands, and Israel, mine inheritance!"[31]

My brothers and sisters, is not all this what the Eucharist images forth for us, its very meaning and promise? The Eucharist is "summons and stimulus" to mission, because it proclaims the death of the Lord, until He comes! There on the cross, God reigns, *regnavit a ligno Deus*, God draws all men to Him!

But is not the Eucharist also "fulfillment of mission"? For at the Lord's table all evangelization reaches its term, at the banquet where all are brothers and sisters, where God's love embraces all the peoples' the dream we all dream, the dream of Catholicity, the dream of *catholica unitas!*

Where else but in the Eucharistic assembly is this final messianic banquet symbolized, promised and in measure already realized? Where, but here, my brothers and sisters, around the meal of the Lord's body and blood, do all the nations of the world assemble, poor and rich, high and low, of every race and color and costume, of every age in the great history of humanity, in all the wondrous diversity of traditions and cultures, amid all the incredible richness of their gifts of mind and heart, and hands and voices, of their very souls...?

Here we hear Blessed Angela of Foligno's prayer, "May your love embrace all the nations!"[32] and Methodius of Olympus, "The Church is in the pains of childbirth until all the peoples shall have entered into her."[33]

---

[31] Is 19:25.

[32] Cf. De LUBAC, H., *Catholicism*, p. 123.

[33] *Ibid.*

In the Eucharist this great prayer and longing is fulfilled. "Already", and yet, "not yet". In every Eucharist, the Kingdom comes already, and yet we still await the fulfillment of the divine mercy, in Augustine's splendid vision, "gathering up the fragments from every side, forging them in the fire of love, and welding into one, into the new Adam, all that has been broken and scattered."

My brothers and sisters, forgive me if this conference has not gathered all the fragments! There was too much to be said, and only this poor Archbishop from a small and distant land to say them: from the land which, over 400 years ago, missionaries came in sailing from this country and albeit accompanied by less noble-minded conquistadores, brought the faith by which my people still live, by which they rejoice and suffer, the faith by which they die into the communion of saints: *La fe de Filipinas es como un sol ardiente!* But the time given me I have used up already, so I must come to the end.

Evangelization as proclamation, as dialogue, as inculturation; evangelization as communion "across all human boundaries"; evangelization as expectation of the great Messianic Banquet at the end of times: evangelization all these, is it not Eucharist which is both "summons and fulfillment", promise and presence? And is not this really what we experience here, as "we lift up our eyes and see, looking all about us", the coming-to-be of that amazing blessing, where upon each one, and upon each people falls that amazing grace whereby each of us, and every race and nation among us, hear our own name, sounded in the symphony of the spirit which is Church, Eucharist and promise of the Kingdom to come: LISTEN!

Blessed be Spain, my people, Russia, Somalia, Bolivia, China, the work of my hands [...] and (if I may give my heart's cry a this moment of rejoicing) Blessed be you, Filipinas, Filipinas, My inheritance! Amen! Amen!

THE SOCIAL CHALLENGE FLOWING FROM SHARING IN AND ADORING THE EUCHARIST

Sister Juana Elizondo Leiza
Superior General of the
Daughters of Charity

Introduction

At the beginning of this talk I beg you to excuse me for having accepted to deal with this theme which would be better treated by others more competent than I. Perhaps I have been, unconsciously, drawn to it by my conditioning as a Daughter of Charity, a servant of the poor and witness of the enormous misery and injustice which is the lot today of a great part of humanity.

Indeed, the geography of poverty grows each time greater in extent and immeasurable proportions in breadth and width from North to South whenever we allow our planet earth to deteriorate.

Amid the fine avenues and skyscrapers of rich cities we find vast ghettos of marginalized people, who are excluded and ill-treated by a selfish and self-sufficient society — a society which while bent on prosperity, comfort and wasteful squandering is quite insensitive to those great many darkened and anguished faces which are without anything attractive at present and without the hope of looking forward to a better future.

In the desolated and dried-up countries of the South sheer misery takes on a variety of different guises and vast proportions.

As the Holy Father, Pope John Paul II reminded us in the opening address of the Conference of Bishops at San Domingo (no. 15):

> The world cannot remain unaffected and smug before the chaotic and alarming situation which meets our gaze: nations, whole sectors of populations, families and individuals ever richer and more privileged in contrast to peoples, families and a multitude of persons crushed by poverty, victims of hunger and disease and deprived of adequate housing, health services, and cut off from human culture. All this is a poignant testimony to a real state of disorder and institutionalized injustice, which are increased often by delaying to take the necessary means, apathy and shameless disregard for ethical principles in carrying out the administrative duties, such as in the case of corruption.

Whereas humanity has never had so many resources, never have so many people experienced such scandalously great a lack of the very necessities for subsistence. While at the tables of the rich there is sheer extravagance, waste and destruction of tons of food, at those of the majority there are not enough scraps...

We can "look" casually and "pass by" the disconcerting real plight of so many people who "are treated

140

like animals", in the words of Saint Vincent de Paul, that prophet of the poor. We can "hear" the cry of so many poor and contemplate like insensitive spectators what we read in the newspapers or see on T.V. — chilling scenes of so many human beings exiled from their countries, wandering homeless and on the run for their lives.

Can we become accustomed to live with injustice without experiencing any sense of reponsibility to correct it? And, in such a situation how can we celebrate the Holy Eucharist, the mystery of communion with God and our brothers, the sacrament of brotherhood, source of love, channel of solidarity and reconciliation?

The sacrament of the Eucharist involves us in building a world reflecting the goodness of the Creator. God has created the world for mankind. All have a right to the earth's goods and resources.

We are called to be a brotherhood — without barriers which prevent an equitable distribution of necessities for all. In Pope John Paul II's Encyclical Letter on the 20th anniversary of Pope Paul VI's *Populorum progressio:*

> Thus, part of the *teaching* and most ancient *practice* of the Church is her conviction that she is obliged by her vocation — she herself, her ministers and each of her members — to relieve the misery of the suffering, both far and near, not only out of her "abundance" but also out of her "necessities"[1].

---

[1] John Paul II, *Concern for the Social Order*, no. 31, Éditions Paulines, 1988, p. 63-64.

Merely to accept and allow the status quo of injustice and inequality between people to continue, without trying to correct it, this is truly a scandal that gives little credibility to the followers of Jesus and is tantamount to "invalidating" the celebration of the Eucharist, sacrament and sign of brotherhood.

1. The divorce between faith, worship and life, a scandal confronting evangelization

A lack of consistency between faith, worship and life is one of the major problems from the most ancient times regarding mankind's relationship with God its Creator.

Is it enough for us to believe in God, to relate to him directly in worship? Or, must we also recognize our fellow human beings?[2] God himself has made his will clear to us in this matter in both the Old and New Testament. The Creator does not allow us to forget our brothers — above all those whom we meet in need.

In the Old Testament we find, first of all the prophets, who made the "voice of the poor" of their times heard in their protests and denounced the unjust situations of those who considered themselves superior to the rest because of their belief and fidelity to certain ritual practices and offering of sacrifices. Among these prophets the following examples are worth recalling:

---

[2] [The Spanish word "semejantes" can mean both "fellows" and also "likeness", which suggests Gn 1:27 regarding being created in God's image and likeness. — Translator's note.]

Amos stands out as a great defender of the poor and oppressed. He was familiar with the economic system of his time and its widespread abuses — which favoured the acquisition of riches through exploitation of the poor — and fearlessly denounced and cried out against the system of injustice, and an empty and sterile kind of worship without good works. He insisted that in carrying out his ritual requirements a believer should also join the practice of justice and mercy:

I hate, I despise your feasts, and I take no delight in your solemn assemblies. Even though you offer me your burnt offerings and cereal offerings, I will not accept them, and the peace offerings of your fatted beasts I will not look upon. Take away from me the noise of your songs; the melody of your harps I will not listen to. But let justice roll down like waters, and righteousness like an ever-flowing stream[3].

There had also already been the prophet *Isaiah's* challenging words:

What to me is the multitude of your sacrifices? says the Lord; I have had enough of burnt offerings of rams and the fat of fed beasts; I do not delight in the blood of bulls, or of lambs, or of he-goats. When you come to appear before me, who requires of you this trampling of my courts? Bring no more vain offerings; incense is an abomination to me. New moon and sabbath and the calling of assemblies — I cannot endure iniquity and solemn assembly. Your new moon and your appointed feasts my soul hates; they

---

[3] Am 5:21-24 [Scripture references in the RSV translation.].

have become a burden to me, I am weary of being them. When you spread forth your hands, I will hide my eyes from you; even though you make many prayers, I will not listen; your hands are full of blood. Wash yourselves; make yourselves clean; remove the evil of your doings from before my eyes; cease to do evil, learn to do good; seek justice, correct oppression; defend the fatherless, plead for the widow. Come now, let us reason together, says the Lord: though your sins are like scarlet, they shall be as white as snow; though they are red like crimson, they shall become like wool[4].

Isaiah condemns cultic worship as something detestable if it seeks to cover up injustices. God cannot accept it if it hides crimes. God's mercy and pardon call for a change of attitude: to seek rights, protect the oppressed, care for the orphan, defend the widow. Come now, let us reason together. Though your sins are like scarlet, they shall be as white as snow[5].

This change of attitude presupposes, above all, a new relationship with the poor and those who are utterly defenceless and neglected.

Other texts of similar forcefulness could be cited from the Old Testament to demonstrate God's will... It is useless to pin one's hope on deceptive ritual. God detests this hypocrisy. God seeks justice — consistency between life and worship, a life-style in accordance with the faith that is proclaimed. This severe condemnation of cultic sacrifice is deserved if it is used as an excuse not to practice the basics of human responsibility and elementary justice — especially

---

[4] Is 1:11-18.
[5] Cf. Is 1:17-18.

towards the weak. The severe challenge presented is to a radical conversion so that our life translates into practice our beliefs and so that it corresponds to our faith. The opposite would be the greatest hypocrisy — that is, it would be to live a lie because of deceiving one's neighbour who is scandalized by one's lack in consistency.

In the New Testament God reveals to us his identification with human beings with whom he seeks to be reconciled — above all with those who are suffering. In the mystery of the Incarnation he makes himself entirely similar to human beings, resembling them in all things except sin. His identification with mankind is complete. He makes himself one with us, whom he raises to the state of "children of God"[6] and considers whatever is done to the least of his brethren as done to himself. To love God is not a matter of theory nor restricted to ritual, but presupposes love shown towards one's neighbour, expressed in deeds. Saint Matthew highlights the deeds that Jesus' disciples must undertake to build up the Kingdom:

Preach as you go, saying, "The Kingdom of heaven is at hand." Heal the sick, raise the dead, cleanse lepers, cast out demons. You received without pay, give without pay[7].

This is what God expects of the Christian's living faith: that he show practical concern for his brother's needs. By this love we shall be judged at the end of

---

[6] 1 Jn 3:1.
[7] Mt 10:7-9.

our lives. Saint Matthew also describes this for us in a dramatic way:

> Then the King will say to those at his right hand, "Come, O blessed of my Father, inherit the kingdom prepared for you from the foundation of the world; for I was hungry and you gave me food, I was thirsty and you gave me drink, I was a stranger and you welcomed me, I was naked and you clothed me, I was sick and you visited me, I was in prison and you came to me." Then the righteous will answer him, "Lord, when did we see you hungry and feed you, or thirsty and give you drink? And when did we see you a stranger and welcome you, or naked and clothe you? And when did we see you sick or in prison and visit you?" And the King will answer them, "Truly I say to you, as you did it to one of the least of these my brethren, you did it to me." Then he will say to those at his left hand, "Depart from me, you cursed, into the eternal fire prepared for the devil and his angels; for I was hungry and you gave me no food, I was thirsty and you gave me no drink..."[8]

Again we see that God regards whatever is done to the neighbour as done to himself and whatever is omitted in regard to the least of his brothers as an insult to him.

Saint James also explicitly states the necessity for consistency between faith and living. He presents with clarity the classic theme of the relationship between faith and works:

---

[8] Mt 25:34-42.

What does it profit, my brethren, if a man says he has faith but has not works? Can his faith save him? If a brother or sister is ill-clad and in lack of daily food, and one of you says to them, "Go in peace, be warmed and filled", without giving them the things needed for the body, what does it profit? So faith by itself, if it has no works, is dead. But someone will say, "You have faith and I have works." Show me your faith apart from your works, and I, by my works will show you my faith. You believe that God is one; you do well. Even the demons believe — and shudder. Do you want to be shown, you foolish fellow, that faith apart from works is barren? Was not Abraham our father justified by works, when he offered his son Isaac upon the altar? You see that faith was active along with his works, and faith was completed by works, and the scripture was fulfilled which says, "Abraham believed God, and it was reckoned to him as righteousness; and he was called the friend of God. You see that a man is justified by works and not by faith alone. And in the same way was not also Rahab the harlot justified by works when she received the messengers and sent them out another way? For as the body apart from the spirit is dead, so faith apart from works is dead[9].

The saints understood clearly the incompatibility in separating the love of God from love of the neighbour and they expressed this doctrine in their lives which were entirely dedicated to others.

Allow me some remarks concerning my Founder, Saint Vincent de Paul, who knew how to express with simplicity the solid theological basis of the practice of

---

[9] Jm 2:14-26.

charity to the humble peasants who constituted the first communities of the infant Company and whose purpose was to serve Christ in the poor:

> To serve the poor means to serve Jesus Christ. My daughters, how true this is! You serve Jesus Christ in the person of the poor. And this is as true as we are here. A sister will go ten times each day to see the sick and then ten times daily she will meet in them God [...] To see the poor condemned criminals in the galleys, will be to meet God; to serve those children will be to meet God. My daughters, this should fill us with so much gratitude! When you go to the poorest house, you meet God there. My sisters, again, this should fill us with so much gratitude! Yes, God welcomes with joy the service which you offer to the sick and receives it as done to himself[10].

Saint Vincent did not understand how a Christian could show indifference to a neighbour's suffering :

> To be a Christian and behold a brother afflicted without weeping with him nor experiencing oneself at one with him in his infirmity — this is to be lacking in charity. It is to be a Christian in name only! It is to lack humanity; it is to be worse than the animals[11].

On many occasions he compared the love of God with service of one's brethren: "Let us love God,

---

[10] Conference to the Daughters of Charity — Saint Vincent de Paul, *Complete Works* [*Obras Completas*, Ed. Sigueme, Salamanca, 1972, IX 1, p. 240].

[11] Conference to the Priests of the Mission, *Ibid.*, IX 4, p. 571.

brothers, let us love God, but let it be with the strenght of our arms... with the sweat of our brow."[12]

He unhesitatingly recommended that if necessary the Sisters should leave their prayer to attend to the poor, because then it would be a question of "leaving God to go to God."[13]

Contemporary theology speaks of the poor as a *"locus theologicus"*. If God is the God of the poor, the poor are his theological dwelling-place. They are to be the place where God manifests himself in a special way, since the Father has chosen it like this[14]. God seeks to be recognized in this theological place; in Jesus, God shows himself to us in an unmistakable way as the God of the poor. God makes himself present in the poor. The poor are a sacrament of God.

Here again, we find ourselves before the great mystery of God's presence in the poor. What a mysterious presence! It coexists with the injustice of which they are victims, at the hands also of the faithful. An imperceptible presence of God, which at the same time both liberates and saves. A baffling presence of God in the poor: suffering with them and showing himself as one who cannot bring such evils to an end.

To be more exact, he shows himself as someone who does not intervene in history, manipulating it from outside forcefully or in sending legions of angels, but he assumes the whole burden of its struggle and overcomes suffering "from within" by *confronting evil with the unique force of solidarity in love*. In the words of

---

[12] *Ibid.*, p. 733.

[13] Conference to the Daughters of Charity, *Ibid.*, IX 1, p. 297.

[14] *Diccionario Teologico "El Dios cristiano"*, Secretariado Trinitario, Salamanca, p. 1112.

Gonzáles Faus: "the silence of God does not mean that God does not intervene in the world, but that he presents a challenge by his call and gift of love and his loving invitation."[15]

Does God not seek our involvement in this theological situation where we find his anguished presence? Do we employ all our energies to reduce the sufferings of others? According to Evely: "God only needs our hands to offer a remedy to the evils of the world."

But there is not only suffering and crucifixion among the poor. God is present there in their midst, in their anguish; he is also present in certain seeds of resurrection which can be discerned as visible in their faith, courage, patience in suffering, hope and confidence in a better future.

Does God not also want us to know how to discern these tiny seeds of resurrection, and to encourage and foster their development by using the means he has entrusted to our hands?

All that is required of us is that we take pains to discover the poor in the light of faith and make our "option for the poor with a preferential love." The first step will be to throw oneself energetically into this task, so that we become incarnated in this reality and wholly filled with compassion through and through in all that we are and have; we must denounce every injustice and its roots; we must seek to transform the structures which generate unjust poverty. Our own liberation from attachment to wealth will give us the strenght to denounce injustices and proclaim the

---

[15] *Ibid.*, p. 1113.

Gospel. Solely by starting from a *consistency between the faith we profess and our way of living it out,* shall we have *credibility.* The best argument in defence of Christianity is that, Christians practice what they profess, become in deeds what they believe.

Not without sadness do we hear the reproach (rightly or not) made by young people especially: "We believe in God, but not in the Church nor in you because you do not do what you say."

Certain negative aspects of our life can become an obstacle for those who are seeking truth and desiring to be converted.

We cannot remain unaware of the Church's repeated invitations which the Holy Father has issued — such as in his Encyclical Letter *Centesimus annus,* which commemorates the centenary since *Rerum novarum:*

> For the Church the social message of the Gospel must not be regarded as a theory, but first of all as a basis and motivating force for action. Spurred on by this message, some of the earliest Christians distributed their goods to the poor. In this way they witnessed that despite social differences it was possible to live together peacefully united. Strengthened by the Gospel in the course of the ages monks cultivated the lands; religious (both men and women) founded hospitals and homes for the poor; confraternities (embracing men and women of all social classes) committed their members to care for the needy and marginalized; their conviction sprang from Christ's words: "Whatever you do for one of these, my least brethren, you do unto me" (Mt 25:40). This did not remain abstractly at the level of a pious intention, but became expressed in concrete living commitment.

Today more than ever the Church is aware that its social message will find credibility primarily in the *witness of deeds,* rather than in its coherence and inner logic. From this conscientious awareness springs its preferential option for the poor — a decisiveness of direction which is never exclusive nor discriminatory towards other groups.[16].

2. Christians, christian community and transformation of society

In his proclamation of the Good news to humanity Jesus wants to count on the simple people of the earth. He calls some in a special way: the twelve apostles and the seventy-two disciples; but, according to the account of the evangelists, there are the multitudes who follow him to listen to his words and become witnesses of his works.

To be a Christian is a gift, a grace, a vocation. It means following Christ, clinging to him, "to be his", to be like him, to do what he did. Living the Christian vocation signifies sharing in a process of belonging, holding on to and identifying with Christ. This process is begun at baptism, strengthened at confirmation, fulfilled at the Eucharist. A Christian who fully lives his faith is:

— a new man — "born of water and the Spirit"[17];

— a witness of Christ, who has chosen to live the values of the kingdom in the spirit of the beati-

---

[16] *Centesimus annus,* no. 57.
[17] Jn 3:5.

tudes, which foster the renewal and transformation of persons and society;

— a person of communion, who lives in love with God and his brethren, expressing this love in the whole of his existence and actions.

A person begins at baptism a new life as a Christian when Christ communicates his Spirit to him and brings about his transformation: "You were washed; you were sanctified; you were justified in the name of the Lord Jesus Christ and in the Spirit of our God."[18]

Living in the state of the "new man" signifies sharing not only in the message of the Gospel, but a radical conversion, an entire gift of oneself to Christ who completely changes one's life; it means stripping off the "old man" in order to put on the "new man"; it requires dying to sin and living for God in Christ Jesus:

> Let not sin therefore reign in your mortal bodies, to make you obey their passions. Do not yield your members to sin as instruments of wickedness, but yield yourselves to God as men who have been brought from death to life, and your members to God as instruments of righteousness[19].

The task of being a Christian consists in resembling Christ, that is, making him real today. A Christian must be a visible historical sign of Christ's presence in the world. When renewed by the Spirit and imbued with his strength and grace, he is enabled to witness

---

[18] 1 Cor 6:11.
[19] Rm 6:12-13.

to God before mankind and to be, like leaven, a catalyst of *social transformation*.

The transformation of the world begins already with the converted Christian whose approach and dealings with other persons and things deeply expresses again in this world the life of a son of God moved by a new spirit[20].

To be a Christian is to be a person of communion. This means living the reality of eucharistic brotherhood which unites a believer to the whole Christ: to live in communion with Christ and one's brethren. To receive the body of Christ, to say "Amen" to Christ, is also to acknowledge one's brethren, to say "Amen" to the Church, to the community:

Since you are the body of Christ and members of Christ, the sign of your mystery *(symbolo)* is before you on the holy table. You yourselves acknowledge this by responding: Amen. To what is said to you: "the body of Christ", you reply: "Amen, so it is." Be, therefore, members of Christ in order that your reply may ring true[21].

To live in communion realizes brotherhood, which implies accepting and respecting others, mutual sharing and love, surrender of self at the service of all. Through communion Christians contribute to the transformation of society... to bring about a more humane world where there is justice, solidarity,

---

[20] Cf. *Testigos del Dios vivo*, p. 36 (Witnesses of the living God).

[21] Cf. Saint Augustine, *Sermon 272*.

peace, love. Such a world of brotherhood is already here on earth the beginning of the Kingdom of God.

Even though we are living in a time of rapid communication, which is brought about through highly sophisticated technology, many persons feel lost and isolated in the midst of the swirl of an anonymous mass of people. Paradoxically it is possible for a person to remain isolated without being able to be alone! The human person is created for communion with others and through them with the Creator.

God himself is the deep mystery of communion in his intimate being: for the eternal relation of three Divine Persons expresses the perfect solidarity of communion in Being. The Son of God, who is nearest to the Father's heart, has revealed to us how God is a trinitarian communion. In his death and resurrection he reveals God as his Father and the Person of the Holy Spirit whom he gives us on behalf of the Father as a font of life, love and filial communion: this spiritual life of communion unites us as children of the Father and brothers of Christ and all mankind. It is above all on the Cross that God reveals himself as a Trinity of Persons in perfect unity by surrendering and being surrendered in love.

The mystery of the Divine Being which is revealed in Jesus is a mystery of love, communion, personal relationship. In God there exists one COMMUNITY, the original and prototype Community which is the font and model of all community life. Jean Daniélou describes the trinitarian communion in this way:

Here is one of the points at which the mystery of the Holy Trinity throws much light on human living. We are taught that the very depth of existence, the basis of what is real and what establishes everything is love experienced in a community of persons [...] The very basis of the Christian revelation is the fact that the divine persons in their reciprocal bonds and mutual communication have a primary and absolute importance: the fact of this same communication of the divine persons is the basis itself and the archetype of all reality — that pattern to which everything must conform. We understand for this reason that human communion derives from the trinitarian communion. All reality is summed up in that "all may be one as we are one."[22]

Furthermore, God wanted to enter into a communion of love with mankind by means of manifesting the design of his love in the divine revelation. He wished to dwell in the midst of a people so that mankind would find itself united with him in communion and by means of communion:

I shall put my spirit within you, and cause you to walk in my statutes and be careful to observe my ordinances. You shall dwell in the land which I gave to your fathers; and you shall be my people, and I will be your God[23].

God created people to live in communion with one another: "male and female he created them"[24] so that they would discover the meaning and path of their

---

[22] DANIÉLOU, Jean, *La Trinidad y el misterio de la existencia*, Ed. Paulinas, Madrid, 1967, p. 54 ff.

[23] Ezk 36:27-28.

[24] Gn 1:17.

life in community and solidarity. Jesus determined the pattern of communal life in calling the apostles to share with him an evangelical style of living and by forming with them the apostolic community: "he called to him those whom he desired; and they came to him. And he appointed twelve, to be with him, and to be sent out to preach."[25]

The first Christians likewise established themselves in community. The Acts of the Apostles describe the extraordinary life of the first Christian community in Jerusalem. In it there was true KOINONIA, which was a community united with Christ risen from the dead; in him it was united with the Father and with the brethren through the power of the Holy Spirit. Jesus' disciples "devoted themselves to the apostles' teaching and fellowship, to the breaking of bread and the prayer."[26] They shared a *communion of goods*: "all who believed were together and had all things in common"[27]; "no one said that any of the things which he possessed was his own"[28]; "they sold their possessions and goods and distributed them to all, as any had need"[29]; "there was not a needy person among them, for as many as were possessors of lands or houses sold them, and brought the proceeds of what was sold and laid it at the apostles' feet; and distribution was made to each as any had need."[30]

However, in the community of Jerusalem there was not merely a "sharing of goods", but also a

[25] Mk 3:14.

[26] Ac 2:42.

[27] Ac 2:44.

[28] Ac 4:32

[29] Ac 2:45.

[30] Ac 4:34-35.

"*sharing of hearts and souls.*" When Saint Luke speaks of "one heart and soul", he is certainly referring to the diversity of persons who made up these communities. Their differences sprang from their background, age, education, occupations, etc. Despite all this they lived so profound a love that they considered themselves "one" — united in a communion of life with God the Father, whose children they all are, and with God the Son, whose brethren they are, one in the Holy Spirit of Love.

The Church is also essentially a mystery of communion and a sacrament of unity, a community of believers, a new people of God, "which proceeds on her pilgrim course between the persecutions of the world and God's consolations."[31]

The Christian community is built up on the Eucharist. It is the Spirit who realizes this union of all in Christ — as the *Epiclesis* invocation of the Eucharistic Prayer brings out. The Christian community is an accomplishment of Christ's grace in mankind, which, following the first community, must be:

— a community of believers, who are joined in prayer, celebrating and sharing faith, nourished by the Bread of the Eucharist[32];

— a community of brethren, who are united in the same purpose, intention and action, loving one another and being of mutual assistance; living in solidarity and justice as brothers who share every-

---

[31] Saint Augustine, *De civ. Dei*, XVIII, 52.2 ; PL 41, 614 — cited in *Lumen gentium*, no. 8 (end).

[32] Cf. Ac 2:42.

thing they possess in common so that no one remains in poverty or inequality[33];

— a community of witnesses, who are sent into the world to be its salt, light, leaven, in proclaiming the Gospel of Christ[34].

The history of the Church witnesses to how it has always given importance to the formation of Christian communities. Among these we can single out those Institutes of consecrated life, which through the ages have been characterized by their radicalism and which, according to their particular charisms, have been and are a leaven not only of evangelization, but also of transformation and social development. Responding to historical needs and local circumstances, they have been and are committed to fostering culture, justice and the practice of charity.

Nor have there been lacking in society some attempts, in keeping with certain ideologies, to create communities in imitation of Christian ones, whose values they have been aware of, although in neglecting those of Christ and the influence of the Spirit these attempts have collapsed. The document of Puebla presents this observation while describing the characterictics of a Christian community:

Each ecclesial community [...] ought to endeavour to be [...] an example of coexistence where freedom and solidarity manage to come together [...] where authority is exercised in the spirit of the Good Shepherd; where a different attitude is taken to wealth;

---

[33] Ac 2:44-45.
[34] Cf. Ac 1:8.

where there are attempts to organize opportunities and structures for sharing which open a way of developing a more human kind of society; and, above all, where it is clearly evident that, without radical communion with God in Jesus Christ, any other kind of merely human communion in the long run results in failure and fatally turns out to be against mankind itself[35].

The Christian community today has a great importance as a focus of credibility in modern society. In the new evangelization to which the Holy Father emphatically urges us to be committed, the witnessing to community is indispensable; such a witnessing signifies a faith which is responsible in transforming reality:

People of our time — and especially youth — need to see in the Christian community the sign of a *reconciling community*, one which is just, joyful, quite new and different insofar as it helps them to believe in God and seek in him what is genuine and fulfilling for their lives[36].

The community which lives and celebrates the Eucharist must make sure that Christ lives and grows in it; that each time again with the disappearance of all that is not communion there is a growth in love, brotherhood, etc. The Eucharist is then the leaven of renewal and of personal and communal transformation.

---

[35] *Document of Puebla*, no. 273.

[36] *Testigos del Dios vivo*, p. 37 (Witnesses of the living God).

A witness of Christ and communion, as a new person, offers hope of being different in Christ's style of living. His lifestyle and pattern of acting are shaped by the spirit of the Beatitudes so that his attitudes and deeds radiate love, truth, peace, justice, forgiveness... This way of relating to others is noted for its simplicity and thankfulness, regard for sharing and an attitude of humility and mercy: "Owe no one anything, except to love one another; for he who loves his neighbour has fulfilled the law."[37]

The Christian community will be more credible and contribute to the *transformation of society* if it strives to express with might and main:

— a "style" of life which offers an alternative to that in the consumer society where "having" holds priority over "being";

— a simple and unostentatious lifestyle which recognizes the proper measure of things in relation to fundamental values... a way of living that prefers improvement of the quality of being to possessing more, giving instead of grasping... sharing all one's possessions... Such a lifestyle has a beautiful humanizing influence in an environment where everything is evaluated in terms of money, profit or usefulness.

Likewise the Christian community will be more credible and contribute in a more effective way to bringing about social change by its constant concern and *preferential care for the poor and needy* through an

---

[37] Rm 13:8.

attitude and activity expressing self-dedication, service and solidarity.

It is precisely by developing the efforts to remain with them and share their conditions of life, as we experience God calling us through our brothers' needs, that the change is brought about in the whole of society so that it becomes more just and welcoming of the poor[38].

The Christian community has to:

— strengthen itself to construct a new society wherein injustices and oppression, fear and terror are rooted out;

— put itself at the service of others in continual self-dedication;

— transform the anti-culture of fear into a culture of life.

It has to do the impossible so that mankind may live with dignity and experience its reconciliation as children of God. It has to fill the emptiness and shallowness in human hearts without showiness... offering motives which sustain them to live in hope.

May God grant that we come to understand the transforming force which drives the Christian community to become a vital expression of the Gospel. Utopia? Excessive radicalism? The one who came to show us to follow his way by the witness of his own life cannot demand anything impossible.

---

[38] *Testigos del Dios vivo*, p. 37 (Witnesses of the living God).

3. Participation and adoration of the Eucharist, source of grace for mission and witness

In obedience to the Father, Christ does not leave us alone in the task of continuing his mission. He entrusts this task to the whole community of the Church and to each Christian so that his work for the salvation of the world is carried on in accordance with each one's particular charism, vocation or ministry.

Since the Eucharist is the living presence of Christ at the heart of the Church, it is the central focus of the mission that the Church has received by the Lord. As the Second Vatican Council puts it: "The Eucharist is the source and summit of the whole Christian life."[39]

In the Eucharist Christians encounter all the energy required to live out faithfully the significance of their baptism. Participation in and adoration of the Eucharist express the source of grace for undertaking their mission as witnesses of the Gospel. Christians cannot leave the eucharistic celebration as those who have beheld a spectacle in virtue of the gift of faith. Their sharing in the Eucharist must not be limited merely to the fulfilment of a duty. The Eucharist forms and commits them to live the Gospel in all aspects and circumstances of human experience.

The first fruit of sharing in the Eucharist is the *transformation of the participants*:

The *penitential rite* invites purification from whatever may prevent Christians becoming united and identified with Christ.

The *offering of bread and wine*, those "fruits of the earth and the work of human hands" which are trans-

---

[39] *Lumen gentium*, no. 11.

formed into the Body and Blood of Christ through the words: "this is my body which will be given up for you [...] my blood which will be poured out", as well as Jesus' invitation: "Do this in memory of me" — all this signifies the Lord's challenge to us to become converted into his Body and Blood so that our only life consists no longer in living for ourselves, but for him whose life we share, in surrendering ourselves entirely with him and in becoming the servants of all our brothers and sisters. We are thus constantly impelled to live in an attitude of self-sacrifice — the gift of the whole of our being.

Communion or participation in the eucharistic banquet — in response to Jesus's invitation: "Take and eat [...] take and drink" — *identifies* us with Christ. We can indeed say with Saint Paul: "it is no longer I who live, it is Christ who lives in me."[40]

Christians who are identified in this way with Christ are the principal agents of the *transformation of society* because their life is an extension of the significance of the Eucharist. Everything that they celebrate and contemplate in the Eucharist becomes, as it were, the agenda which authenticates the sense of purpose and value to which their lives are committed: love-charity, justice-solidarity, equality-unity... Following Christ's example, Christians express through their generous and free dedication of themselves at the service of all, especially the poorest and those most in need, the reality of the sacrifice they offer at Mass.

The whole Eucharist — *prayers, readings, eucharistic prayer* — calls for and challenges us to show consistency between liturgy and life.

---

[40] Gal 2:20.

The Prayer of the Faithful opens us to the widest dimensions of the Church's motives in praying for the world: peace, accidents involving many people, natural disasters, every kind of suffering afflicting our brothers and sisters (particularly among the poor, weak or oppressed...). In our daily lives we cannot remain insensitive to these needs which are gathered up in our intentions at prayer. They should deeply bring home to us the urgency of making an appropriately practical response to each particular situation of need.

The collection enables the faithful to fulfil their responsibilities in solidarity with society by sharing with the needy not only from what they have left over, but also in sacrificing their own ordinary needs. When properly motivated, it helps the faithful to become alert to his social condition and to the bonds of brotherhood he must establish with all mankind even at the cost of sacrifices affecting his own lifestyle.

Sensitivity to one's responsibility of solidarity presents an enormous challenge, which *the Eucharistic Prayers* implicitly take into account in imploring God the Giver of every good thing for the gift of unity, brotherhood...

> We thank you for counting us worthy to stand in your presence and serve you. May all of us who share in the body and blood of Christ be *brought together in unity* by the Holy Spirit...[41]

> Look with favour on your Church's offering, and see the Victim whose death has reconciled us to yourself. Grant that we, who are nourished by his body and

---

[41] Eucharistic Prayer II [ICEL translation].

blood, may be filled with his Holy Spirit, and *become one body, one spirit in Christ*[42].

And that we might live no longer for ourselves but for him[...][43]

This clearly states that one who lives for Christ lives for his neighbour, his brother.

Most poignantly forceful of all are the words of this eucharistic prayer:

Fill our hearts with compassion in confronting human misery; inspire us to offer the appropriate deed and word to a lonely and despairing brother; help us to be available to anyone who feels exploited and abused. Grant that your Church, Lord, become a haven of truth and love, freedom, justice and peace, so that all may discover in it encouragement and energy to go on living in hope[44].

Others (whether Christian or not) expect that what they see Christians celebrating in the Eucharist may be expressed in their lives. With good reason, therefore, they rebuke us harshly when this does not happen — when the beauty of the Eucharist is betrayed!

Our ideals and actions, as sublime as they may be, such as sharing in the Eucharist, lose their value if they are not translated into life through the practice of justice and charity, especially in regard to those most in need.

---

[42] Eucharistic Prayer III [ICEL translation].

[43] Eucharistic Prayer IV [ICEL translation].

[44] Eucharistic Prayer V b) [ICEL translation].

Saint John Chrysostom reminds us that the altar of the Eucharist is also found when we encoutner the altar of the poor:

> You show respect for the altar upon which you place the Body of Christ. Yet, you insult and despise a person in need who is likewise part of Christ's Body. You can find this altar anywhere — in every street, in all the public squares — and you can at any time offer on this altar a true sacrifice[45].

The Eucharist does not end when the liturgical celebration concludes. After the celebration Christ remains present in the consecrated hosts in the tabernacle. The Church does not cease to *adore his presence* in the Blessed Sacrament.

Adoration of the Blessed Sacrament extends the significance of the Eucharist into living. In the words of the Basic Text of the Eucharistic Congress of Seville:

> Adoration is likewise a sign of solidarity with the needy and deprived of the whole world, who are remembered in prayer. This prayerful bond strengthens a sense of justice and brotherhood[46].

As the Church has gone on discovering the riches of the gift of the Eucharist by prayerfully reflecting on it down the ages, it has deepened its devotion towards this Sacrament — encouraging this devotion in visits or silent adoration, in communal worship with exposition and benediction, processions, eucharistic congresses, etc. Whatever the form our devotion

---

[45] In Ep. ad Cor., Hom. 20:3.
[46] Cf. *Christus Lumen Gentium*, no. 25 (g).

takes, it is always meant to lead us to become *intimately united and at one with the Crucified and Risen Christ*, who is present and acting in our midst. What the Eucharist requires of us is that the "Amen" of our faith and love may realize (that is, make real) Christ's saving work in his Church. The Eucharist is the fulfilment of this great work of redemption.

Pope John Paul II in his Encyclical Letter, *Sollicitudo rei socialis* (on Social Concern), reminds us of the *implications* of the Eucharist. The Eucharist makes the Church realize its mission; it sends us out to be missionaries, to evangelize, that is, to offer the world the good news of its *transformation*:

> Thus the Lord *unites us with himself* through the Eucharist — Sacrament and Sacrifice — and he *unites us with himself and with one another* — by a bond stronger than any natural union; and thus united, *he sends us* into the whole world to bear witness through faith and works, to God's love, preparing the coming of his Kingdom and anticipating it, though in the obscurity of the present time. All of us who take part in the Eucharist are called to discover, through this Sacrament, the profound *meaning* of our actions in the world in favour of development and peace; and to receive from it the strength to commit ourselves ever more generously, following the example of Christ, who in this Sacrament lays down his life for his friends (cf. Jn 15:13). Our personal commitment, like Christ's and, in union with his, will not be in vain but certainly fruitful[47].

---

[47] *Concern for the Social Order*, no. 48, Éditions Paulines, 1988, p. 106-107.

In reality this vision is not restricted to events that make the headlines in the news, but it is especially realized in the situations of daily living which are permeated by the implications of justice, charity and brotherhood. In the words of the Second Vatican Council:

> [...] [Christ] reveals to us that "God is love" (1 Jn 4:8); he teaches us that the fundamental law of human fulfilment and hence of the transformation of the world is the new commandment of love. He assures those who believe in divine charity that the way of love is open to all, and that the effort to establish universal brotherhood is not a vain effort. At the same time he warns us that this charity is not to be cultivated only in great matters but primarily in everyday circumstances [...] The gifts of the Spirit are various. He calls some to bear **witness** clearly to the desire for heaven [...] Others he calls to devote themselves to serving humanity here [...] To all he brings liberation, that setting aside self-interest and directing all earthly resources to human purposes, they may reach out towards a future in which humanity itself will become an offering acceptable to God. As a pledge of this hope and as nourishment for this journey, the Lord left us that sacrament of faith in which natural elements cultivated by human beings are turned into his glorious Body and Blood, the supper of brotherly communion, the foretaste of the heavenly banquet[48].

---

[48] *Gaudium et spes*, no. 38 [slightly revised translation from CTS Do 363, p. 36 ff.].

In this context allow me to refer again to Saint Vincent de Paul, that great advocate of frequent communion at the height of the Jansenist age. On the 18th of August 1647 he addressed the Daughters of Charity as follows:

> Someone who has made a good communion has done everything well [...] Such a person will certainly not be acting on his own accord, but only on behalf of Jesus Christ [...] his speech will resemble the meekness of Jesus Christ; he will face obstacles and difficulties with the patience of Jesus Christ. In a word, all his actions will no longer be those of a mere creature; they will be the actions of Jesus Christ[49].

Conclusion

The Church, and every Christian, is associated and involved in Christ's saving mission. An important part of this mission — as we have seen — is the *social transformation* of the world in which we are living. As the Holy Father says in his Encyclical Letter *Sollicitudo rei socialis*, the Church has no technical solutions to offer in solving the enormous problems of this world, nor economic or political systems or programmes; on the contrary, it accepts all those which respect human dignity.

> But the Church is an "expert in humanity", and this leads her necessarily to extend her religious mission to the various fields in which men and women expend their efforts in search of the always relative

---

[49] Cf. *Complete Works*, Éd. Sigueme, IX 1, p. 309.

happiness which is possible in this world, in line with their dignity as persons[50].

The Eucharist, the supreme expression of Christ's love for humanity, situates Christians at the very heart of history and challenges them to undertake the responsibility of building up a new world — a civilisation of love. Christians cannot remain aloof from such a task, but are bonded ever more deeply through love in the struggle of the rest of humanity in such a way that:

> The joy and hope, the sorrow and anxiety of the people of our time, especially of the poor and of those who are in any way suffering; the Christ's disciples make their own, and there is nothing human that does not find an echo in their hearts[51].

In the celebration and adoration of the Eucharist the Church encounters the great teachings of Christ which focus and shape its own *policy for action: love, service, sacrifice, total dedication.* Whereas we are accustomed to speak colloquially of sharing in the transformation of society in such terms as: cooperation, solidarity, justice. These words only become effective insofar as they are animated by Christ's love which leads to a service of our brothers unto the point of total self-sacrifice.

The Eucharist if for Christ's disciple the font from which he can draw the necessary strength to fulfil the sublime, though demanding, mission which the

---

[50] *Concern for the Social Order*, no. 41 [*loc. cit.*, p. 87 — quotation from Paul VI, *Populorum progressio*, no. 13)

[51] *Gaudium et spes*, no. 1 [*ibid.*, p. 7].

Master has entrusted to him. In the Eucharist, Christ is the focal-point of all — of all cultures and levels of knowledge. What is of crucial importance is that we strive to seek him in faith, to open ourselves to his warming light, to welcome the energy which he bestows in order that we are enabled to radiate it as his witnesses and messengers among all our brothers.

May Mary, whom God involved in the redemptive mission of his Son, who is the Mother of all people, and with special tenderness of those in greatest need, help us to discern the great mystery of Christ's Love in the Eucharist and like her, respond faithfully to what the Spirit wishes to accomplish through us in the Church and in the world.

Achevé d'imprimer
en janvier 1994
sur les presses de
Imprimerie Métrolitho Inc.

Imprimé au Canada — Printed in Canada